W9-BNX-386

DATE DUE

Sharpening

otoshop CS2

Real World Image Sharpening with Adobe Photoshop CS2

Industrial-Strength Production Techniques

Bruce Fraser

Real World Image Sharpening with Adobe Photoshop CS2

Bruce Fraser

Copyright ©2007 by Bruce Fraser

Peachpit Press
1249 Eighth Street
Berkeley, CA 94710
510/524-2178
Fax: 510/524-2221

Find us on the Web at www.peachpit.com.

Peachpit Press is a division of Pearson Education.
Real World Image Sharpening with Adobe Photoshop CS2 is published in association with Adobe Press.

Interior design by Stephen F. Roth/Open House
Cover Design: Aren Howell
Cover Illustration: Ben Fishman, Artifish, Inc.

ISBN 0-321-44991-6
9 8 7 6 5 4 3

Printed and bound in the United States of America

Overview

The Big Picture

Contents

What's Inside

Preface

Real World Sharpening

For the past fifteen-plus years, I've labored in the vineyards of Photoshop, coaxing pixels to do my will. In that time, I've seen huge advances in the handling of tone and color. When I started doing digital imaging, getting the image to look the same on two different monitors was a major break-through, and matching the print to the screen appearance was the stuff of which science fiction was made. Nowadays, it tends to be the rule rather than the exception.

We've made gargantuan strides in the handling of tone and color, but when it comes to control of *detail*, which is what this book is really about, we're still in 1991. It's just about impossible to make two different displays render image sharpness the same way, and predicting print sharpness from the display is an exercise fraught with pitfalls and perils. In fact, we're back in the days of, "If you want to know what it will look like when you print it, print it, then look at it."

As a result, sharpening (and the equally important other side of the coin, noise reduction and smoothing) tends to be an ad hoc practice. We flail around until we get something that looks decent on the display and hope that that appearance will somehow be transferred to the printed piece.

Photoshop CS2 offers many powerful features for handling image detail. But how do you know what to aim for? This book contains a plethora of different sharpening tricks and techniques, but perhaps the most important contribution it tries to make is to provide you with an analytical framework that lets you think about sharpening in a new way. When we sharpen, we have to take at least three things into account:

▶ The relationship between image detail and system noise that's imposed by the capture medium—we want to sharpen image details but we don't want to exaggerate film grain or digital noise.

▶ The requirements of the image content—the wrong kind of sharpening can exaggerate texture we'd rather downplay, or even obscure detail instead of emphasizing it.

▶ The needs of the print process—when we translate pixels into marks on paper (or canvas, or any other substrate on which we care to print) we inevitably introduce some softness for which we try to compensate by sharpening.

The huge problem is that these needs often contradict one another.

The Sharpening Workflow

The solution is the sharpening workflow. By treating each demand separately, we can assure that all are addressed optimally. To some, this may smack of heresy. Doesn't everyone know that you can only sharpen an image once? I hope that this book demonstrates that multipass sharpening is not only feasible, but optimal. It's simply impossible to address all the conflicting needs of image source, image content, and output process in a single round of sharpening.

That said, multipass sharpening demands care and attention. Blasting images with multiple hits of sharpening can easily create a hideously oversharpened mess, which is why the conventional wisdom dictates that you only sharpen once. The techniques described in this book will allow you to sharpen images safely, and optimally.

The sharpening workflow confers another benefit. By separating sharpening for output from the other sharpening processes, it creates use-neutral master images that you can easily repurpose for different output processes, at different sizes and resolutions.

Sharpening and the Display

One of the hardest sharpening lessons to learn is that what you see on your computer screen can be highly misleading. But the screen display is often all you have to rely on for your judgments.

Some display technologies render images much more sharply than others—the same image almost invariably looks sharper on an LCD display than it does on a CRT. Display resolution also has an impact. I've gone to some lengths to debunk the polite fiction that computer screens display images at 72 pixels per inch, and have even given instructions that will let you determine the real resolution of *your* display, which is the one that really matters.

But the most important lesson of all is that good sharpening for print can often look terrible—really, hideously, horribly bad—on screen. Learning the relationship between what you see on *your* display and what shows up on hard copy is a vital skill to acquire.

Objective Realities

Some parts of the sharpening equation are determinate. Human visual acuity—the ability to discern fine details—has limits that are rooted in the physiology of the eye. The same visual properties that we exploit to produce the illusion of continuous tone from dots of four colors of ink also have a direct bearing on sharpening.

Print sharpening is also a determinate process. Any given print process will always translate pixels into dots in the same way, regardless of image source or image content, so for any print process, there's a right answer in terms of sharpening. (Of course, there's also a very large number of wrong ones.)

Creative Capacities

But sharpening is also a creative tool. We use sharpening to emphasize important detail (and sometimes we use blurring to suppress irrelevant, distracting detail), to make a point, to tell a story, to invoke an emotion, to provide an illusion of three-dimensionality in our two-dimensional photographs.

The sharpening workflow has a place for creativity too. But it's important to know when to be creative, and when to go by the numbers!

Who Needs This Book?

If you work with images that are destined for hard copy, and you aren't totally confident about all your sharpening decisions, my hope is that you'll find this book beneficial. No matter whether you make your own prints, send them out to an online printing service, or deliver commercial work destined for offset press, the sharpening workflow can help you get the most out of your images.

This is not a book for Photoshop beginners, but neither is it a book only for Photoshop experts. Some of the techniques described herein use fairly esoteric Photoshop features with which you may or may not be familiar. Don't let that put you off. I've yet to encounter a piece of software that was smarter than its users, and Photoshop is no exception. Almost all the techniques in this book are nondestructive—they don't touch your original pixels—so you can't do any harm to your images by trying them.

How the Book Is Organized

I've tried to present all the information you need to build your own sharpening workflow in a logical manner.

The first two chapters look at the technical underpinnings of sharpening. Chapter 1, *What Is Sharpening?*, looks at the fundamental nature of sharpening—what it does, and how it works. Chapter 2, *Why Do We Sharpen?*, discusses the need for sharpening, and all the factors we need to address when we sharpen.

Chapter 3, *Sharpening Strategies*, provides an overview of the sharpening workflow, and shows how it addresses each sharpening phase. Chapter 4, *Sharpening Tools and Techniques*, is the tactical complement to Chapter 3. It describes the various tools and techniques that the sharpening workflow employs.

Chapter 5, *Putting the Tools to Work*, shows how to use the tools and techniques described in Chapter 4 to satisfy the goals outlined in Chapter 3 by building a sharpening workflow from initial sharpening, through creative tweaking, all the way to final output.

Chapter 6, *Case Studies*, shows examples of the sharpening workflow in action, dealing with different types of images from different sources, to demonstrate the flexibility and power the workflow offers.

A Word to Windows Users

This book applies to both Windows and Macintosh. But I've been using Macs for over 20 years, so all the dialog boxes, menus, and palettes are illustrated using screen shots from the Macintosh version. Similarly, when discussing the many keyboard shortcuts in the program, I cite the Macintosh versions. In every shortcut cited in this book, the Command key translates to the Ctrl key and the Option key translates to the Alt key. I apologize to all you Windows users for the small inconvenience, but because Photoshop is so close to being identical on both platforms, I picked the one I know and ran with it.

A Necessary Disclaimer

Much of the material in this book is an outgrowth of work that I did in the process of developing a commercial sharpening tool, PhotoKit Sharpener, from PixelGenius LLC. I'm proud of PhotoKit Sharpener, but while it embodies all the philosophy and many of the techniques I've described here, it isn't what this book is about. I recognize that automated solutions based on someone else's presets, no matter how well thought-out, aren't for everyone.

Image Credits

I'm indebted to Jeff Schewe for the use of his striking copyright image which appears in multiple locations in Chapters 5 and 6, and for his JPEG images in Chapter 2; to Seth Resnick, for the portrait of me that appears on page 94; to Stephen Johnson, for the portrait of me that appears on page 216; and to Christiane Reitz for the scary cat picture featured in Chapter 6. All the other images, such as they are, are my own.

Thank You!

I couldn't have written this book without help. My first votes of thanks go to Pam Pfiffner at Peachpit Press for provoking me into writing the book, and to Thomas Knoll, for creating Photoshop and thereby giving me something to write about.

Victor Gavenda, my editor, made my prose look polished; production virtuoso Lisa Brazieal turned my virtual creation into a manufactured reality; Liz Welch corrected my many typos and inconsistencies—any that remain are entirely my fault. Karin Arrigoni provided the index to make sure that everyone can find the information they need.

Thanks to my pals and partners in Pixel Genius LLC—Martin Evening, Seth Resnick, Andrew Rodney, and Jeff Schewe, for being the finest bunch of people with whom it has ever been my pleasure and privilege to work, and for challenging me to put what I thought I knew about sharpening into practice. An even bigger vote of thanks goes to the late Mike Skurski, who passed away in October 2005, and without whom I would never have been able to produce a successful software product. We all miss you. And thanks to the Pixel Mafia—you know who you are!

And as always, I thank my lovely wife, Angela, for being my best friend and partner, for supporting me in all my activities, and for making my life such a very happy one.

Bruce Fraser
San Francisco, June 2006

1

What Is Sharpening?

And How Does It Work?

An old saw in photography goes, "If you want great prints, use a tripod!" While it's usually delivered half-jokingly, the important grain of truth is that one of the ways our brains try to make sense of the world as seen by our eyes is by breaking the scene down into edges and non-edges. If the edges in an image appear too sharp or not sharp enough, our brains tell us that there's something wrong, and the image appears unconvincing.

Sharpening is arguably one of the most important yet least understood aspects of digital image reproduction. Examples of badly sharpened images are easy to find—you probably need look no further than your daily newspaper. Good sharpening, on the other hand, is invisible.

Sharpening can't fix sloppy focus or insufficient depth of field. What it can and should do is to make sure that the sharpness of the original capture is carried through faithfully to the final output. Of course, sometimes we also use sharpening to improve reality—we may add some extra snap to the eyes and hair in a head shot, for example. But the primary purpose of sharpening is *not* to rescue overly soft images, but simply to counteract the inevitable softening that happens when we turn photons into pixels and pixels into marks on paper.

In Chapter 2, we'll look at the various factors that give rise to the need for sharpening, but before we examine those, let's look at how sharpening works, whether it's done in a wet darkroom using analog tools, or accomplished digitally either in the camera or in Photoshop.

1

Emphasizing Edges

Sharpening works by increasing the contrast around edges. Edges in images always involve darker tonal values adjacent to lighter ones. We can emphasize the edges by making the dark tonal values darker and the light tonal values lighter.

In the analog darkroom, this was accomplished using an *unsharp mask*—see the sidebar, "Why Is It Called Unsharp Mask When It's Used to Sharpen?" for details on just how this process worked. In the digital domain, we sharpen by identifying the dark and light pixels that represent edges, and lowering the value of the dark pixels to make them darker while raising the value of the light pixels to make them lighter.

When we do this, we create a "halo" that makes the edges, and hence the entire image, seem sharper. The concept is simple, but as with many things in digital imaging, the devil is in the details that we discuss throughout this book!

Figure 1-1 shows the same image before and after sharpening. (The image also illustrates the pitfalls of driving in rural Scotland—a good metaphor for the myriad things that can go wrong when we use sharpening inappropriately!)

Figure 1-1
**Before and
after sharpening**

unsharpened   *sharpened*

The only difference between the two versions is the sharpening. Figure 1-2 shows a zoomed-in comparison with an accompanying graph of the values of a single row of pixels, before and after sharpening.

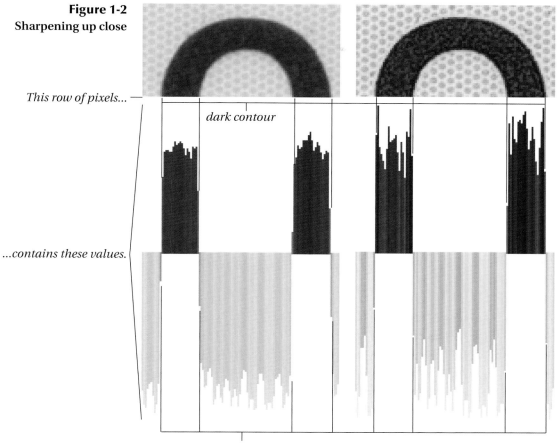

Figure 1-2
Sharpening up close

This row of pixels...

dark contour

...contains these values.

light contour

Notice that the tonal range of the sharpened version—the distance between the lightest and darkest tones—is wider than that of the unsharpened version. Notice too that the biggest differences occur at the edge transitions of the capital "O" while smaller differences emphasize the texture of the sign's background.

Sharpening is closely related to contrast, but simply increasing the contrast over an entire image just produces an over-contrasty image. Successful sharpening demands that we localize the contrast boost to those parts of the image that actually represent edges.

Why Is It Called Unsharp Mask When It's Used to Sharpen?

Sharpening predates digital imaging by decades. If you've often wondered why one of Photoshop's main sharpening tools is named the "Unsharp Mask" filter when it's supposed to make the image sharper, rest assured that you're not alone.

The name originates in an analog wet darkroom technique. It increases the apparent sharpness of a photographic print using a duplicate of the negative to create a mask that increases contrast along the edges.

The original and the duplicate negatives are placed on either side of a piece of glass—often just plain old window glass—and the entire sandwich is placed in the enlarger's negative carrier.

When the enlarger is focused on the bottom negative, the top, out-of-focus copy creates a contrast mask that boosts the contrast along the edges in the image as the out-of-focus dark contour burns the dark side of the edges and the out-of-focus light contour dodges the light side of the edges.

The technique is called "unsharp masking" because the mask—the top, out-of-focus negative—is out of focus and hence isn't sharp. In short, it's an unsharp mask that has the effect of increasing the apparent sharpness in the print!

So the "unsharp" in "unsharp mask" refers to the mask, not the result, and it's this analog technique that Photoshop's Unsharp Mask filter replicates (only with a great deal more control than its analog counterpart!)

Analog Roots

As a photographic practice, sharpening has its roots in the analog world, as the sidebar above indicates. However, the analog unsharp masking technique described therein offered only two controls.

▶ The distance between the two negatives (the thickness of the glass) controlled the width of the sharpening halo.

▶ The exposure time controlled the strength of the contrast boost.

The limited control and uncertain results prevented unsharp masking from becoming a mainstream practice in analog photography. But it did see some use in sharpening analog color separations for offset printing, often by making a blurred duplicate of the continuous-tone separation, then printing it together with the sharp version as a contact print, after which the separation was screened.

Sharpening for continuous-tone photographic prints was something of a luxury, but when the continuous-tone original was turned into cyan, magenta, yellow, and black dots of ink, some of the original sharpness was lost. So sharpening became, and remains to this day, a standard operation in prepress. When the drum scanner replaced the stat camera, digital sharpening became the norm.

Digital Sharpening

Digital sharpening tools offer much more precision, control, and wealth of options than the analog darkroom ever did. The inevitable downside is that with greater control comes greater responsibility, and the more options on offer, the more opportunities for mistakes, as we'll demonstrate throughout this book.

But in the switch from optical to digital reproduction (and eventually to digital capture) it quickly became clear that whenever we turn photons into pixels, and pixels into marks on paper, we need to sharpen the image, otherwise it will appear unacceptably soft. There are simply no exceptions to this rule. The questions, to which the rest of this book is devoted to providing answers, are when to sharpen, what techniques to use, and how much sharpening to apply.

However, there's one key difference between digital and analog sharpening with which we have to contend in varying degrees, and that's the handling of noise. Analog sharpening rarely increased noise, and often had the effect of reducing it, because the mask was made from a different piece of film than the original, and hence the distribution of the film grain—the main noise component in film images—was different. This had the desirable effect of making the noise in the mask cancel out the noise in the original. With digital sharpening, we aren't so lucky.

Digital Noise Reduction

When it comes to digital sharpening, noise reduction is the other side of the coin. Sharpening tools such as Photoshop's Unsharp Mask filter evaluate one pixel at a time, determining how different it is from its neighbors. If the difference is great enough, the filter decides that this pixel represents an edge, and adjusts its value accordingly.

The inherent problem is that the computer has no way of knowing whether the pixel differences represent real image information or noise, so unless we take steps to prevent it, most sharpening routines emphasize the noise as well as the edges. If you refer back to Figure 1-2 earlier in this chapter, you'll see that the capital "O" in the sharpened version of the image is much noisier than in the unsharpened one.

However, if you refer even further back to Figure 1-1, it's unlikely that you'll see any objectionable noise in the print. The noise is confined to dark tones in small areas. Figure 1-3, on the other hand, shows what can happen if we fail to take noise into account.

Figure 1-3
Noise problems

*This version of the
image had noise
reduction applied before
sharpening, and had
sharpening applied
through a mask.*

*This version of the
image was simply
sharpened globally,
emphasizing noise as
well as detail.*

This image is something of a worst-case scenario, shot at ISO 1600 under aquarium lighting on a fairly noisy digital SLR. But it dramatizes the point that we must take noise into account when we sharpen if we don't want our images to appear like sandpaper.

In many cases, we can prevent the sandpaper simply by protecting the noisy areas from sharpening, but in extreme cases like the one shown in Figure 1-3, some more proactive noise reduction may be needed before the application of sharpening.

Digital noise reduction is exactly the opposite of sharpening. Instead of increasing localized contrast, it reduces it, thereby rendering the noise less visible or even removing it entirely. Of course, the inevitable catch is that as it reduces the noise, it also de-emphasizes the edges, making the image softer.

So one of the first key skills to master in sharpening is striking the right balance between emphasizing edges and reducing noise, walking the fine line between sharpness and sandpaper. Overly aggressive noise reduction creates an irreparably soft image, so noise reduction must always be used with caution, and should always be done prior to sharpening. Most of the time, simply making sure that we don't sharpen noise does the trick, but when images are captured on high-speed film or at high ISO settings on a digital camera, we may have to do a little more.

Sharpening and Pixels

All digital sharpening is carried out on pixels. Throughout this book, we'll examine images at the pixel level to see what happens to the pixels through various stages of image reproduction. But with the exception of images destined for on-screen display on the Web or in an information kiosk, the final product is not pixels, but marks on paper or some other substrate.

But the relationship between the image pixels and the marks on paper is rarely obvious. In conventional halftone printing—the kind we use on printing presses, it typically takes between two and four pixels to form a single halftone dot in grayscale printing. When we print in color, the relationship is even less obvious since the halftone dots are spread across four different color plates.

Inkjet printers use a different type of screening, but again, the relationship between printer dots is indirect. Even in the relatively simple scenario of printing to a true continuous-tone printer, where the pixels are reproduced one-to-one, the pixels on the print are typically much smaller than the same pixels on screen.

How big are your pixels? We can't control how the pixels get turned into printer dots. We *can* control the degree of contrast boost, and the size of the pixels on output. In so doing, we control, in turn, the width of the sharpening "halo." The goal is to avoid haloes that our eyes pick out as discrete features, while making them strong enough, and (just) wide enough to produce a sharpening effect.

Final sharpening must be done at final output size and resolution.
Since we can only control the final size of the pixels, it follows that we must
do our final sharpening at final output size and resolution if we want to
get the sharpening halo right. If the image is resized after sharpening, the
haloes either get bigger, and become visually obvious, or they become too
small and we lose the sharpening effect.

For some people, that means that *all* sharpening must be deferred until
the image is at output size, otherwise multiple rounds of sharpening will
destroy the image. That's one of the notions this book seeks to challenge:
It's certainly true that multiple rounds of sharpening *can* destroy the image, and it's equally true that the final, critical round of sharpening must
be tailored to the output process and applied to the final image pixels.

But I'll be arguing throughout the remainder of this book that optimal
sharpening simply cannot be accomplished by a single pass of sharpening
at the end of the image preparation process, because the softening that
occurs when pixels are turned into print dots is only one of several, often
competing factors that must be addressed.

In the next chapter, we'll look at all the different factors we need to take
into account when we sharpen.

2 Why Do We Sharpen?

And What Must We Take Into Account When We Do So?

Whenever we turn photons into pixels, we lose some sharpness, because no matter how high the resolution of our capture devices, they sample a fixed grid of pixels, and so they turn the continuous gradations of tone and color that exist in the real world into discrete pixels. When the pixels are small enough, they provide the *illusion* of continuous tone, but it *is* an illusion, and sharpening is one of the things we simply have to do to make the illusion convincing.

The reason that sharpening is such a complex topic (and the reason for this book) is that successful sharpening has to take into account several potentially competing factors. In this chapter, I'll discuss these factors in detail, but they fall into three basic categories:

▶ The image source

▶ The image content

▶ The image use

For decades, the standard operating procedure has been to punt on the question, and try to handle all sharpening in one single pass just before output. With film scans, this worked after a fashion, though I suspect the results were rarely optimal. With most digital captures, the results are even less likely to be optimal simply due to the way most digital cameras work.

Does My Image Need Sharpening?

If your image appears reasonably sharp when viewed at Actual Pixels zoom level on your display, and your intended output is something other than to the display at the size you're viewing, your image needs sharpening.

Of course, if your image appears soft at Actual Pixels zoom level on the display, it needs sharpening no matter what the final use. But one of the harshest sharpening lessons I've learned is that it's extremely difficult to make judgments about output sharpening by looking at pixels on the monitor.

Sharpening and the Monitor

Unless the monitor is your final output, making images look sharp on the monitor almost invariably results in an undersharpened print. But monitors themselves vary hugely in the way they reproduce sharpness.

Monitor technologies. LCD displays are much sharper than CRT displays. An image that looks sharp on an LCD display may still look soft on a CRT. An image that looks sharp on a CRT display may look slightly crunchy on an LCD.

If your images are destined for a specific type of display, for example, a kiosk, you should ideally look at the images on that display before making any final judgments. If your images are being prepared for the Web, realize that you have very little control over what the other billion or so Web users will see.

Nowadays, many more users have LCD displays than have CRT displays. All you can do is to aim for the middle of a very large barn door, but an LCD display is likely to be more representative of the general Web population than is a CRT.

Monitor resolution. The resolution of the display also has a major impact on how we see sharpening. An image that looks pleasingly sharp on a display running at 1600 x 1200 displays obvious, less-pleasing sharpening haloes on the same display running at 1024 x 768. This is simply because the pixels are displayed at a larger size when the display is run at 1024 x 768, so the sharpening haloes become more obvious because they're bigger.

Again, if you're sharpening images for the Web, you need to aim for the "average" condition, which is probably closer to 1024 x 768 than to 1600 x 1200.

The Monitor as Guide

Sharpening for the display is an uncertain endeavor unless you know exactly the display for which you're sharpening. But there's a much bigger issue, which is how to use the display as a guide for sharpening. The easy answer is, unfortunately, that there are no easy answers!

Fortunately, the situation isn't hopeless—it's just challenging. The fundamental concern that should always be foremost in your mind is the actual size of the pixels on output. But to understand the relationship between what you see on the screen and what you get on output, some additional information is useful.

True monitor resolution. Many of us tend to leave unquestioned the polite fiction that computer monitors have a resolution of 72 pixels per inch (ppi). This is often not the case—in fact it's quite unlikely that you monitor's resolution is exactly 72 ppi, though it may be close.

Monitor vendors usually specify the size of the monitor's image area as a diagonal measurement, which makes for a big number but isn't all that useful for figuring the resolution. Determining the true resolution of your monitor is a simple exercise that requires no equipment more complicated than a tape measure.

1. Measure the *width* of the image area on your monitor with the tape measure.

2. Divide that measurement by the number of horizontal pixels your monitor displays.

3. The resulting number is the true resolution of your monitor in pixels per inch (ppi.)

The horizontal image area of both my LCD displays (an EIZO CG 21 and an NEC 2180 WG) is meaninglessly close to 16.875 inches. I run them at 1600 x 1200 resolution, so the actual resolution is 94.8 ppi. (If I were to run them at 1280 x 1024, the resolution would be 75.9 ppi.) The image area on CRTs is more variable than on LCDs because the geometry controls let you adjust the picture size, but my 22-inch LaCie CRT and my 22-inch Sony Artisan both produce resolutions of around 123 ppi when run at 1920 x 1440.

Table 2-1 shows the approximate resolutions for typical display sizes and resolutions.

Table 2-1 **True monitor resolution**	Monitor size	Pixel dimensions	ppi
	21-inch LCD	1600 x 1200	95
		1280 x 1024	76
		1024 x 768	61
		800 x 600	47
	30-inch LCD	2560 x 1600	102
	17-inch laptop	1440 x 900	100
	21/22-inch CRT	1920 x 1440	122
		1600 x 1200	102
		1280 x 1024	82
		1152 x 870	74
		1024 x 768	65
		800 x 600	51

Knowing your monitor's true resolution is key in understanding the relationship between the pixels you see on your display and the final printed results.

If your display is around 100 ppi, and you're printing at around 240 ppi, viewing the image at 50% will give you a truer picture of the final sharpening. It still won't be perfect—Photoshop's downsampling algorithms have a different effect on sharpness than do the mechanisms by which printers or platesetters turn image pixels into dots—but it'll be a lot closer than the Actual Pixels (100%) view.

Likewise, if your display is around 75 ppi and you're printing at 300 ppi, the 25% view will give you a closer idea of final sharpness than any of the higher zoom percentages.

Tip: Avoid Odd Zoom Percentages. The 50%, 25%, and conceivably the 12.5% views preserve sharpness reasonably well, but the odd zoom percentages (66.7%, 33.3% and so on) do not, because Photoshop applies fairly strong antialiasing to those zoom levels, thereby making the image appear softer than it will be on final output.

The key point to all this is that when we look at sharpening on the monitor, we're viewing it "through a glass, darkly" (though the Apostle Paul doubtless had something else in mind when he coined the phrase).

At some fairly far-off future date, we may benefit from some technology that compensates for the large variation in the ways different monitors display the same pixels' sharpness, just as color management currently lets us compensate for the way different monitors display the same pixels' colors, but that day won't come soon.

Until that day arrives, you'll have to learn to make that compensation in your head. This is not trivial, but neither is it impossible. First, you need to understand the size relationship between your pixels on screen and your pixels on output. Then it's a matter of learning the behavior of your display, and making constant comparisons between what it shows you and what ends up in print, so that you gain experience as to what will work and what will fail. Throughout the remainder of this book, I'll provide pointers as to the kinds of things to look for.

Sharpening Issues

The first sharpening issue we have to confront is the inevitable softening that occurs whenever we turn a continuous stream of photons into discrete square pixels. No matter how good our lenses, no matter how high-resolution our digital cameras or scanners, the digitization process always loses some sharpness.

Further softening occurs on output, when we translate image pixels to printer dots. Each output process has its own requirements for sharpening—we need to apply very different sharpening to the same pixels printed at 300 ppi to a continuous-tone printer and at 300 ppi to a 150-line screen halftone printer.

Last but not least are the issues presented by the image content itself. A forest full of trees needs a different sharpening treatment from a head shot of a model. Sharpening that emphasizes the fine detail in the trees turns the model's skin into a moonscape, while sharpening that emphasizes the models eyes and lips may actually obscure the detail in the forest. Somehow, we have to reconcile the various and sometimes contradictary needs of the image source, the image content, and the output process.

I'll spend the rest of this chapter looking at these disparate demands in detail, because until they're understood and addressed, sharpening won't do justice to the image, and may actually harm it more than help it.

Image Sources

The image source imposes its own signature and its own limitation on the image. The signature is the relationship between the noise that we want to de-emphasize, and the detail that we want to emphasize. The limitations are the degree to which the image can be enlarged, and the smallest details that can be captured.

In part, enlargement is limited by the gross pixel count, especially with digital captures, but the noise signature also plays a role—we typically scan film to obtain a significantly higher pixel count than digital captures offer, yet film scans cannot withstand as much enlargement as a digital capture of equivalent pixel dimensions. The reason is that digital captures generally have less "noise" than scanned film, because the interaction between the film grain and the scanner's pixel grid exaggerates the grain to produce a noise signature stronger than the digital noise from digital cameras.

A great deal more heat than light has been generated in discussions of the equivalent information content of digital and film captures. Without adding too much fuel to the fire, my experience tells me that 35mm film scanned at 6300 ppi (creating a file approximately 8900 by 5700 pixels) has about the same potential for enlargement as a digital capture in the 6–8 megapixel range (approximately 3000–3500 by 2000–2350 pixels). This is a very approximate rule of thumb.

Detail, Film Grain, and Scanner Noise

The first sharpening challenge lies in emphasizing detail without emphasizing noise. We can often accomplish this by simply protecting the noisy areas from sharpening. In more extreme cases, we may need to apply some noise reduction prior to sharpening. (I'll discuss specific techniques for doing both in Chapter 4, *Sharpening Tools and Techniques*.)

Much depends on the final use of the image. Downsampling can hide a great deal of noise, making the image easier to sharpen, so for one-off uses at sizes that are small enough to allow downsampling by 50% or more, noise may be less of a concern. But as we approach the practical size limitations of the capture, the noise becomes ever-more obvious and may need special handling. Scanned transparencies, scanned negatives, and digital captures all have their own noise characteristics. They share the property that noise increases with higher ISO ratings, but they differ in important ways too. First, let's look at scanned film.

Transparency film grain. The grain in scanned film becomes visually obvious at scanning resolutions far below that required to resolve individual grains. (Resolving individual grains would require scanning at ridiculously high resolutions of around 11,000 ppi, providing no more usable image information than a lower-resolution scan.)

Grain is most obvious in small formats like 35mm, and much less obvious in medium- or large-format transparencies. However, much of the image noise comes not from the grain itself, but from the interaction of the grain, the scanner's sampling grid, and any digital noise introduced by the scanner.

The grain in color transparencies tends to be monochromatic, but the scanner noise is typically strongest in the blue channel, since the blue filter is the least efficient in terms of allowing light to pass through. As a result, transparency grain often shows up at its strongest in clear blue skies, though close examination of the pixels shows that the grain is present in the other channels, albeit to a lesser extent.

Figure 2-1 shows three views of typical scanned transparency noise.

▶ The first view is an attempt to show the actual image pixels, printed at 72 pixels per inch. Note, however, that the grain on screen actually looks worse than the grain in print due to the softening effect of the halftone process.

▶ The second view is a "contact print" that reproduces the actual scanned pixels at 300 pixels per inch, the optimal resolution for the 150-line screen with which this book is printed. This view represents the optimal enlargement one can reasonably attempt from this capture. (On many images, we can drop the resolution to 225 ppi, and hence make a bigger print, but fine diagonal features will usually suffer.)

▶ The third view shows the entire image, still unsharpened, but downsampled to 300 pixels per inch. The image appears reasonably sharp, and more or less grain-free, due to the massive downsampling—the image is now only 16% of the original captured size.

Figure 2-1 also shows the individual color channels at the same Actual Pixels view as the first illustration. It shows how dramatically noisier the blue channel is than the red or green. The purpose of the figure is to convey an impression of typical grain in a transparency scan, and to show its diminishing influence as we reduce the image size.

Figure 2-1
Noise in scanned
transparencies

*This zoomed-in view
shows the unsharpened
pixels from a 35mm
transparency scanned
at 6300 ppi, printed at
72 ppi.*

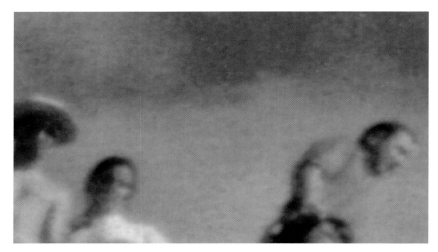

*This view shows a
larger section of the
unsharpened image
printed at 300 ppi to
produce the maximum
size the capture can
support optimally. (The
full-sized image would
be approximately
27 x 19 inches.)*

*This view shows
the entire image
downsampled to 300
ppi, with the zoomed
area above outlined in
black. The image is still
unsharpened, but the
noise is largely rendered
invisible due to the
downsampling.*

Figure 2-1
Noise in scanned
transparencies, *continued*

*This zoomed-in view
shows the unsharpened
pixels from the red
channel.*

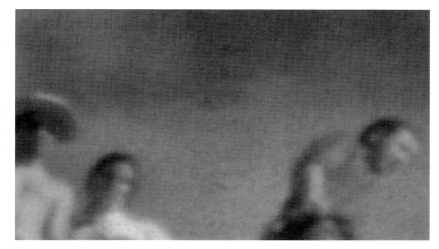

*This zoomed-in view
shows the unsharpened
pixels from the green
channel.*

*This zoomed-in view
shows the unsharpened
pixels from the blue
channel. Notice how
much more obvious the
noise in the blue
channel is compared
to the red or green.*

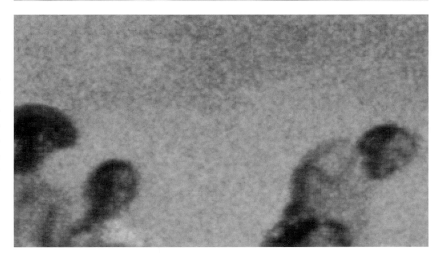

Figure 2-2 shows optimal and less-than-optimal sharpening for the image at "contact print" resolution, and at the downsampled resolution required to fit the image to the page. The optimally sharp versions were created by applying preliminary sharpening and noise reduction selectively using layer masks to isolate the edges, then applying global sharpening tuned to the halftone printing process.

In the case of the downsampled image, the preliminary sharpening and noise reduction for the optimally sharpened version were performed on the full-resolution 6,300 ppi capture, then the image was downsampled

Figure 2-2
Optimal and
less-optimal sharpening

The "contact print" with selective sharpening and noise reduction applied to the high-resolution data before final sharpening. It's a little soft, but bear in mind that the full-sized image would be 27 x 19 inches, so the viewing distance would likely be greater.

The "contact print" sharpened globally shows about the same amount of detail as the version above, but the grain is objectionably obvious in the sky.

to 300 ppi and sharpened for the halftone process. The other version was simply downsampled to 300 ppi, then sharpened globally.

The differences between the two are much more subtle on the downsampled version than they are in the "contact print," reinforcing the point that the final output size makes a big difference, but the globally sharpened version shows some shifts in both tone and hue that are absent in the optimally sharpened version, and the clouds appear a tad crunchy.

Figure 2-2
Optimal and less-optimal
sharpening, *continued*

*The full image with
selective sharpening and
noise reduction
applied to the high-
resolution data, followed
by downsampling and
final sharpening.*

*The full image
downsampled and
sharpened globally.*

Color negative film grain. Grain is typically much more obvious in scanned color negative than in scanned transparencies. It's not that color negative is inherently grainier than transparency. Color negatives record a wide dynamic range from the scene and compress it into a narrow dynamic range on film, and when we scan, we expand that narrow dynamic range recorded on the film. In so doing, we exaggerate the grain more than we do with color transparencies.

As with color transparency, the noise is a product of the film grain, the scanner's sampling grid, and the noise introduced by the scanner, but the noise signature is noticeably different from that of transparency film. Noise in color negatives manifests itself as color noise rather than monochromatic noise, and so demands a different treatment.

Moreover, while the degree to which we have to address grain separately from sharpening depends on the enlargement factor needed, just as it does with transparency film, color negative requires more aggressive treatment, and requires it at lower enlargement factors than transparency.

Figure 2-3 shows the typical noise before sharpening from a color negative scanned at 6300 ppi, using the same views as Figure 2-1:

▶ An "Actual Pixels" view printed at 72 ppi. Again, remember that the on-screen appearance is a little worse than the print you see here due to the softening effect of the halftone process.

▶ A "contact print" view showing a snippet of the image made by printing the captured pixels at 300 ppi—the full-sized image would be around 19 x 27 inches.

▶ The full image downsampled to 300 ppi.

The extreme downsampling to 300 ppi in the bottom image mitigates the grain by downsampling it almost out of existence. But the "contact print" view shows that grain in color negative scans is stronger and a bigger problem than that in transparency scans, and hence requires special handling at lower magnification factors than color transparencies.

As a result, traditional prepress has generally shunned color negatives in favor of transparencies, no matter which film format. Reproducing images from 35mm color negative is certainly challenging, but it's by no means impossible to produce good results even from 35mm. Shooting larger format film reduces the grain problem by reducing the enlargement factor, which is the reason prepress has generally preferred the larger formats.

Figure 2-3
Noise in scanned
color negative

*This zoomed-in view
shows the unsharpened
pixels from a 35mm
color negative scanned
at 6300 ppi, printed at
72 ppi.*

*This view shows a
larger section of the
unsharpened image
printed at 300 ppi to
produce the maximum
size the capture can
support optimally. (The
full-sized image would
be approximately
19 x 27 inches.)*

*This view shows
the entire image
downsampled to 266
ppi, with the zoomed
area above outlined in
black. The image is still
unsharpened, but the
noise is largely rendered
invisible due to the
downsampling.*

Figure 2-4
Channel noise in scanned
color negatives

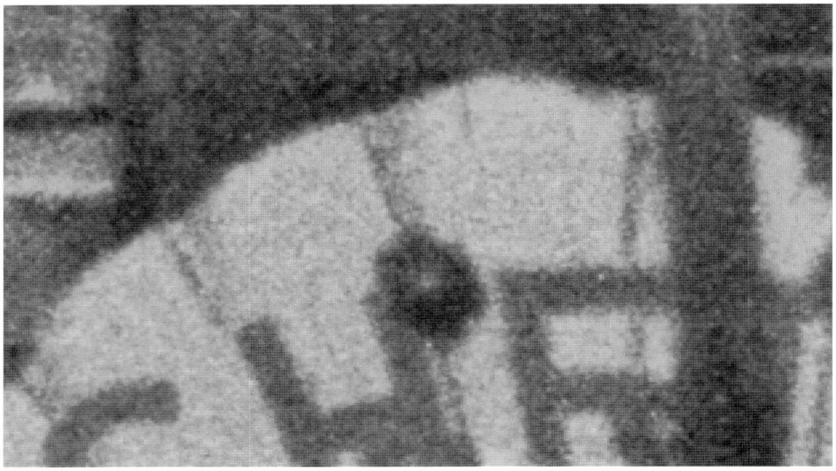

*This zoomed-in view
shows the unsharpened
pixels from the red
channel.*

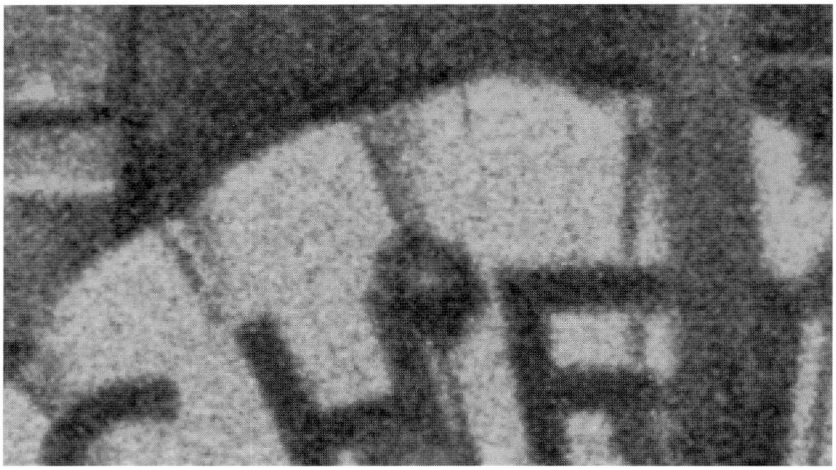

*This zoomed-in view
shows the unsharpened
pixels from the green
channel.*

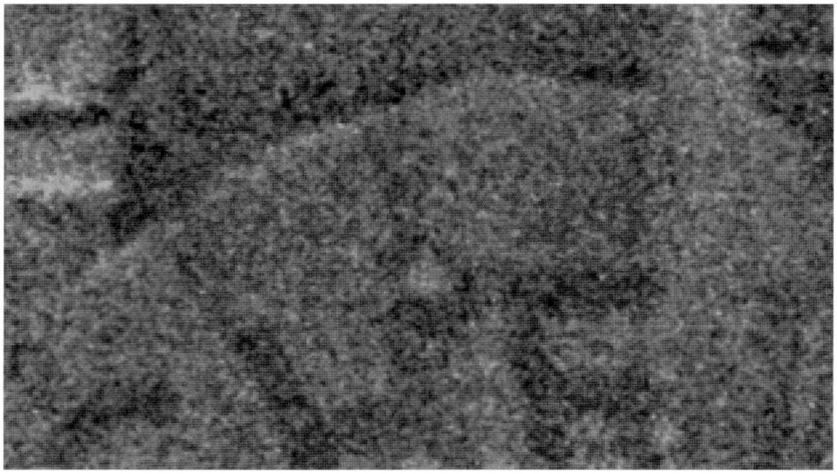

*This zoomed-in view
shows the unsharpened
pixels from the blue
channel. Notice how
much more obvious the
noise in the blue
channel is compared
to the red or green.*

Figure 2-4 shows the actual pixels from the individual channels. Again, the blue channel is the noisiest of the three due to the physics of the scanner, but the color negative shows more noise in the green and blue channels than does the transparency.

Figure 2-5 shows the two versions of the "contact print" and the complete image. The first version of each has had noise reduction and selective sharpening applied through masks, followed by a second round of sharpening tailored to the output process. The second version of each has been sharpened globally at the final output resolution.

Figure 2-5
**Optimal and
less-optimal sharpening**

*The "contact print" with
selective sharpening and
noise reduction applied
to the high-resolution
data before final
sharpening. The full-
sized image would be
20 x 30 inches.*

*The "contact print"
sharpened globally
shows objectionable
grain everywhere.*

Figure 2-5
Optimal and less-optimal
sharpening, *continued*

*The full image with
selective sharpening and
noise reduction
applied to the high-
resolution data, followed
by downsampling and
final sharpening.*

*The full image
downsampled and
sharpened globally.*

With the color negative, the difference between the two versions is more obvious than with the transparency example, even in the downsampled version. The sky is grainier, and the license plate is more difficult to read, in the globally sharpened version than in the version that had noise reduction and sharpening applied to the high-resolution data prior to downsampling. So clearly grain is a more pressing concern with color negative than with transparency, though it again varies with enlargement factor.

Detail, Noise, and Digital Capture

Noise in digital captures differs from the noise in scanned film in several important ways. But before examining the differences in detail, we should point out that several different technologies get lumped into the general category of "digital camera," each with its own properties.

The vast majority of digital cameras, whether point-and-shoot or digital SLRs, are color filter array (CFA) cameras. In a CFA camera, each photosite on the sensor is covered by a color filter and contributes a single pixel to one color channel. The "missing" color information is then interpolated from the neighboring pixels in a process known as demosaicing. Figure 2-6 shows a typical Bayer-pattern color filter array.

Figure 2-6
A typical color filter array

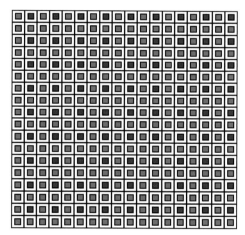

In a Bayer Pattern color filter array, each photosensor is filtered so that it captures only a single color of light: red, green, or blue. Twice as many green filters are used as red or blue because our eyes are most sensitive to green light.

When you shoot JPEG or TIFF, the demosaicing is performed in the camera using the camera vendor's proprietary routines. When you shoot Raw, the demosaicing is done by the raw converter, which typically offers more control.

Demosaicing is a complex process that inevitably involves a trade-off between localized contrast (which looks a lot like sharpening), and anti-aliasing (which looks like blurring), to prevent artifacts that arise when a detail in the image falls on only one color of pixel. Many cameras include an optical low-pass filter to reduce artifacts, but the raw converter, whether in the camera or in post-capture software, performs a significant role, so one raw converter's output with "no sharpening" may appear sharper than another raw converter also set to no sharpening. Similarly, while most raw converters offer some noise reduction, the actual results may differ.

Cameras that shoot JPEG present an additional issue—the nature of JPEG compression creates 8 by 8-pixel blocks that can become visually obvious after editing, or even, at high ISO ratings, before editing. So the challenges presented by digital CFA cameras are quite different from those posed by scanned film. CFA cameras are prone to two distinct types of noise: color noise and luminance noise.

Color noise. All CFA cameras suffer from color noise to a greater or lesser degree—it's an inevitable byproduct of demosaicing. Color noise can raise its head anywhere: it's largely independent of ISO speed or exposure settings, and it can appear in highlights, shadows, or midtones. It does, however, vary from camera to camera. Most raw converters do a good job of eliminating color noise, so much so that many shooters use a "set-and-forget" approach, dialing in a default color noise reduction setting for each camera.

Color noise in JPEGs can be more problematic. The in-camera conversion doesn't always do a good job of eliminating color noise, and the JPEG compression process tends to accentuate any color noise that isn't eliminated in the in-camera conversion.

Luminance noise. Unlike color noise, luminance noise varies both with ISO speed and with exposure. Underexposed digital captures are much more prone to noise, particularly in the shadows, than are underexposed film captures, so it's quite possible that a well-exposed ISO 1600 digital capture may be less noisy than an underexposed ISO 100 digital capture.

Some raw converters, particularly those from the camera vendors, have a tendency to bury shadow noise by simply clipping shadows to black, but it's usually worthwhile addressing luminance noise in the raw converter when you shoot raw. At very high ISO speeds, however, a dedicated third-party noise-removal tool may be needed to get the best rendering.

Luminance noise in high-ISO JPEGs should always be addressed before sharpening, and any remaining noise should be protected from sharpening, otherwise it will simply become more obvious. I'll discuss specific techniques for doing so in Chapter 4, *Sharpening Tools and Techniques*.

Color noise example. Figure 2-7 shows color noise from a digital raw capture made at ISO 100, with good exposure. This image has no significant luminance noise, so this example focusses exclusively on color noise.

Figure 2-7
Color noise in a digital raw capture

This zoomed-in view shows the unsharpened pixels before color noise reduction from a 6.3 megapixel digital raw capture, printed at 72 ppi.

This zoomed-in view shows the same pixels after color noise reduction.

This view shows the image at the 300 ppi "contact print" resolution, with no color noise reduction. (The full-sized image would print at approximately 10.25 by 6.8 inches at this resolution.)

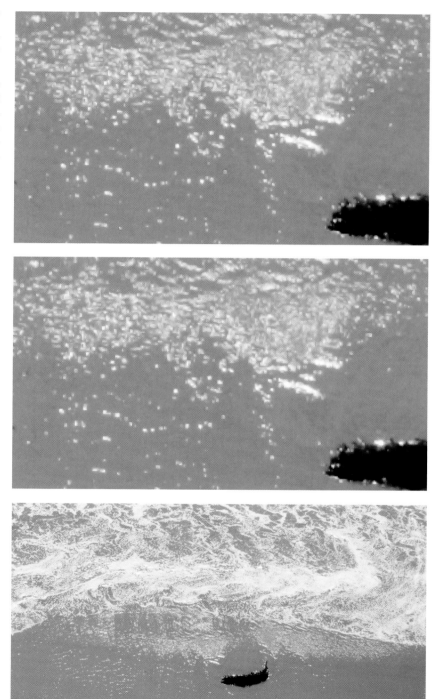

Figure 2-7
Color noise in a digital
raw capture, *continued*

*This view shows
the image at the
266 ppi "contact print"
resolution, after color
noise reduction.*

*The full image,
downsampled to
266 ppi with no color
noise reduction, then
sharpened globally.*

*The full image,
downsampled to
266 ppi with color noise
reduction, selective
sharpening through a
mask, and final output
sharpening.*

At Actual Pixels and contact print zoom levels, the color noise is visually obvious. On the full-sized downsampled image, the color noise is still there if you look for it, but the bigger difference is between the global sharpening and the more nuanced multipass sharpening, which produces much better midtone contrast. We'll return to this topic later, but first let's look at some images where noise is a more significant problem.

Noise and exposure. Figure 2-8 shows Actual Pixels view of a significantly underexposed (-2 stops) raw capture shot at ISO 100. It suffers from much more noise than the ISO 100 image shown in Figure 2-7 because of the underexposure. Where noise reduction was desirable in the image in Figure 2-7, it's essential in the image shown in Figure 2-8!

Note that while the color noise reduction has almost no impact on perceived sharpness, the luminance noise reduction softens the image considerably. We always have to walk a fine line between reducing noise and losing detail. However, in this case, the softening can be rescued by careful sharpening.

Figure 2-9 shows three "contact print" views of the image from which the detail in Figure 3-8 was extracted (the full image would be 10.25 by 6.8 inches). All three have received identical two-pass sharpening. The only difference between the three versions is in the noise reduction.

In Figure 2-9, we've taken care to protect the noise from unwanted sharpening by doing a good deal of selective sharpening through a mask on the first pass. Figure 2-10 makes a different comparison on the same image, showing global sharpening with no noise reduction, global sharpening with noise reduction, and optimal two-pass sharpening with noise reduction.

At the downsampled resolution used in Figure 2-10, the differences are subtle, but if you examine the shadows and midtones carefully you should be able to detect them (and much of this book is about the subtle difference between adequate and optimal sharpening).

What's noteworthy about Figure 2-10 is that, even although the heavy luminance noise reduction required by the underexposed image introduces quite a bit of softening, the detail is easily recovered with careful sharpening. Somewhat less obvious but equally important is the fact that by making good decisions about localized sharpening, we can actually obtain a sharper result with less noise than we can by sharpening globally.

Figure 2-8
Digital noise
and underexposure

The Actual Pixels view of
this underexposed image
shows both color noise
and luminance noise.

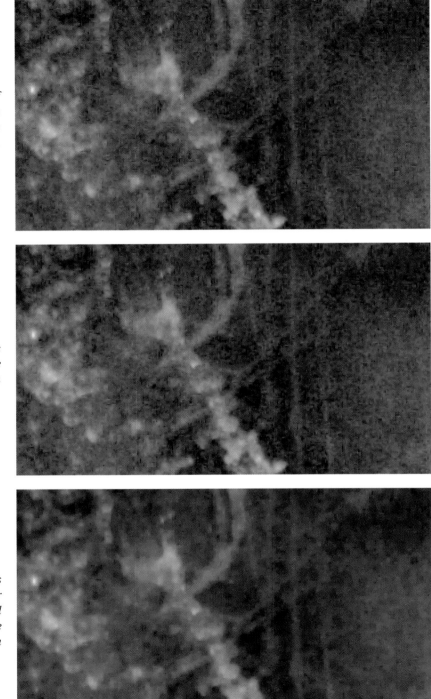

The Actual Pixels
view after color noise
reduction

The Actual Pixels
view after color
noise reduction and
luminance noise
reduction

Figure 2-9
Noise reduction and
sharpening

*Two-pass sharpening
with no noise reduction*

*Two-pass sharpening
with color noise
reduction*

*Two-pass sharpening
with color noise
reduction and
luminance noise
reduction*

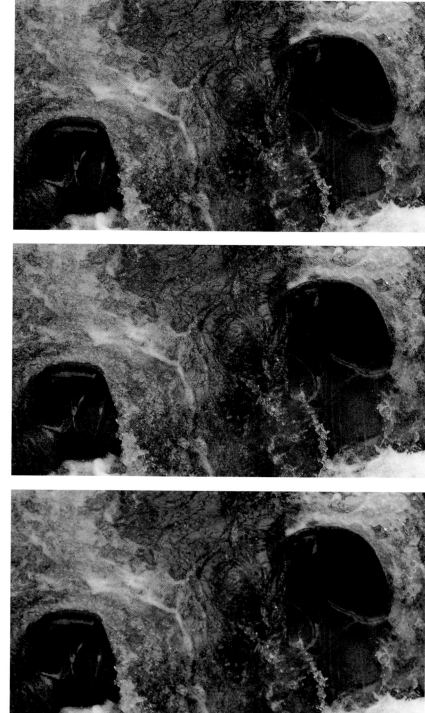

Figure 2-10   Noise reduction and sharpening

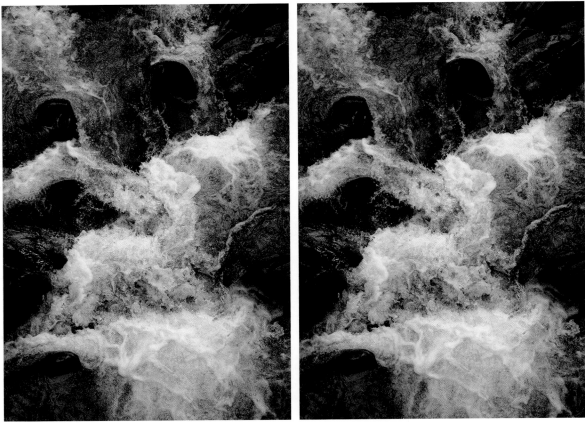

No noise reduction, global sharpening   *Color and luminance noise reduction, global sharpening*

One of the many compelling reasons for shooting raw is the control it offers over the demosaicing process in terms of color noise reduction, luminance noise reduction, and sharpening. The examples I've shown thus far have all shown ideal resolution (where ppi is 2x the line screen frequency) or downsampled resolution. But one of the attractive properties of digital captures is the degree to which they can be enlarged.

Noise, detail, and enlargement. We've seen that the influence of the image source decreases with downsampling. The converse is also true. When we enlarge digital captures past their native resolution, noise

Figure 2-10   Noise reduction and sharpening, *continued*

Color and luminance noise reduction,
two-pass sharpening

reduction and localized sharpening become increasingly more important as the enlargement factor increases.

The degree to which we can enlarge digital captures depends in part on the image content. Images with soft detail can generally withstand more enlargement than those with lots of fine detail. (I'll look at image content issues in greater detail later in this chapter.)

The image shown in Figure 2-11 contains plenty of fine detail, but with care, it can easily be enlarged by 200%. The key is first to apply appropriate noise reduction (the image is relatively clean, but still has some color noise and rather more luminance noise), then to sharpen selectively through a mask before applying final sharpening globally.

Figure 2-11
Noise reduction,
sharpening, and
enlargement

*One-pass sharpening
with no noise reduction
at camera native
resolution*

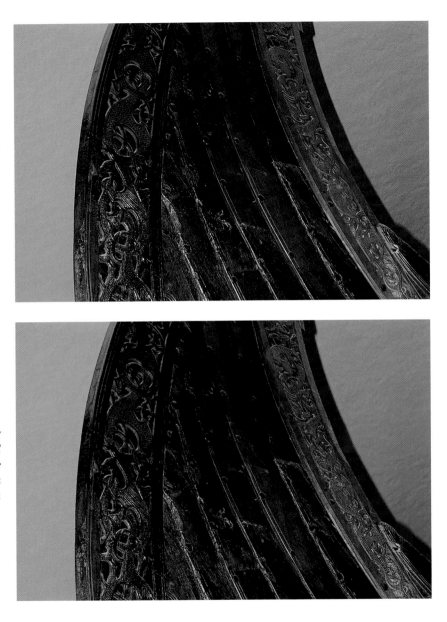

*Two-pass sharpening
with color and
luminance noise
reduction at camera
native resolution*

At the native camera resolution (printed at 300 ppi), the noise in the upper image is only mildly objectionable, though it is noticeable in the darker areas. But a single pass of sharpening that is strong enough to bring out the detail in the lighter wood produces a harsh effect on the highlights. The two-pass sharpening in the lower image reveals the detail in a gentler, more natural-appearing way.

Figure 2-11
Noise reduction,
sharpening, and
enlargement, *continued*

*One-pass sharpening
with no noise reduction
at double the camera's
native resolution*

*Two-pass sharpening
with color and
luminance noise
reduction at camera
native resolution*

When the image is upsampled by 200% (I did the upsampling in Photoshop using Bicubic Smoother interpolation, but a near-identical result is obtained by upsampling in the raw converter), the difference is more obvious. The noise is more noticable in the top image, and it also shows less detail than the bottom version. Digital captures better lend themselves to upsampling than do film scans, but care is needed.

JPEG and noise. When we shoot raw, the raw converter offers a good deal of control over sharpening and noise reduction. When we shoot JPEG, however, we simply have to work with what the camera gives us. Most cameras offer settings for JPEG quality, size, and sharpness, but few if any offer control over noise reduction.

It's much easier to deal with noise that hasn't been sharpened in the camera than it is to de-emphasize it after the fact, so I generally recommend leaving any in-camera sharpening turned off—see the sidebar, "Why Camera Vendors Offer In-Camera Sharpening."

JPEG presents special challenges, not just because of the relative lack of control it offers over raw, but also due to the nature of JPEG compression. JPEG attempts to produce "visually lossless" compression, and at low compression settings (such as the typical JPEG Fine offered by most digital cameras) you may be hard-pressed to tell the difference between a JPEG and a raw capture simply by looking at them side by side. Figure 2-12 shows just such a comparison.

Figure 2-12
Raw and JPEG compared

One of the images at right was shot as a Large Fine JPEG from a Canon EOS 10D. The other was shot as raw from the same camera. Can you tell which one is which?

Why Camera Vendors Offer In-Camera Sharpening

Camera vendors offer in-camera sharpening to play to two very different audiences: Consumers who use point-and-shoot cameras; and pros who are compelled to shoot JPEG for speed reasons.

Most consumers don't have access to sophisticated sharpening tools and techniques like the ones I discuss in this book, and would be dismayed to find that all their images looked softer than those from a point-and-shoot film camera, which their current digital point-and-shoot probably replaced.

Pros who shoot JPEG typically do so because time pressures (both in shooting and in processing) prevent them from shooting raw. Many photojournalists and wedding photographers fall into this category. In-camera sharpening produces reasonable (though hardly ever optimal) results with no user intervention, and thus allows them to deliver their images in a timely fashion.

But in-camera sharpening is a global, one-size-fits-all process. If the final use is small-size reproduction, it may be good enough, but if you want optimal sharpening using the techniques described in this book, and you have to shoot JPEG, I recommend that you turn off sharpening in the camera. Multipass sharpening must be done carefully!

I am indebted to my friend and colleague Jeff Schewe for the images in Figure 2-12, and for the series of JPEG images that grace the following pages. He let me use them on the condition that I emphasize that they constitute an interesting technical exercise rather than an expression of his art, which can be seen at www.schewephoto.com.

The JPEG is the top image in Figure 2-12, the raw is the bottom one. Both were sharpened identically, and printed at 300 ppi. The two versions have small differences in tonality and color balance, but they're extremely similar in terms of sharpness and detail.

However, Figure 2-12 represents something of a best-case scenario. Both images were well exposed and shot at ISO 100. At higher speeds, or with underexposed images, the relative inflexibility of JPEG becomes more apparent, with increased noise and, at higher ISO speeds, some magenta-green color artifacts.

JPEG and ISO speed. JPEG captures shot at low ISO ratings are relatively well-behaved. But at higher speeds, they become progressively more difficult to handle. Figure 2-13 shows JPEGs ranging from 100 to 1600 ISO at "contact print" resolution, showing unsharpened, globally sharpened, and optimally sharpened versions of each.

Figure 2-13
JPEG and ISO speed

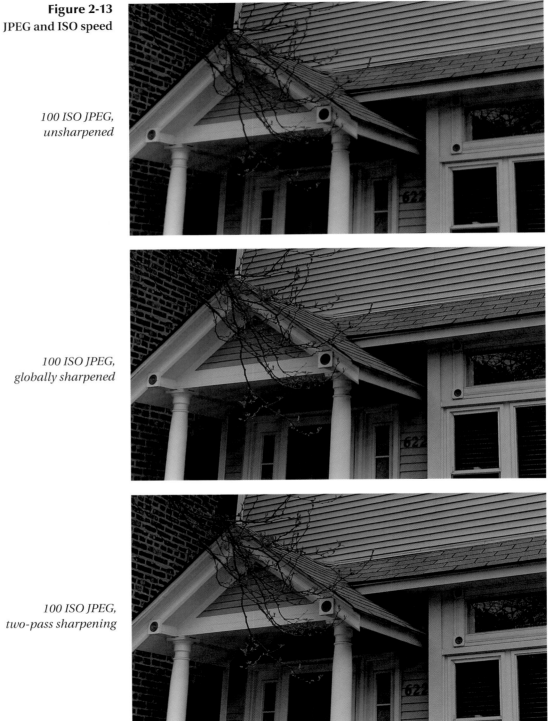

*100 ISO JPEG,
unsharpened*

*100 ISO JPEG,
globally sharpened*

*100 ISO JPEG,
two-pass sharpening*

Figure 2-13
JPEG and ISO speed,
continued

*200 ISO JPEG,
unsharpened*

*200 ISO JPEG,
globally sharpened*

*200 ISO JPEG,
two-pass sharpening*

Figure 2-13
JPEG and ISO speed,
continued

*400 ISO JPEG,
unsharpened*

*400 ISO JPEG,
globally sharpened*

*400 ISO JPEG,
two-pass sharpening*

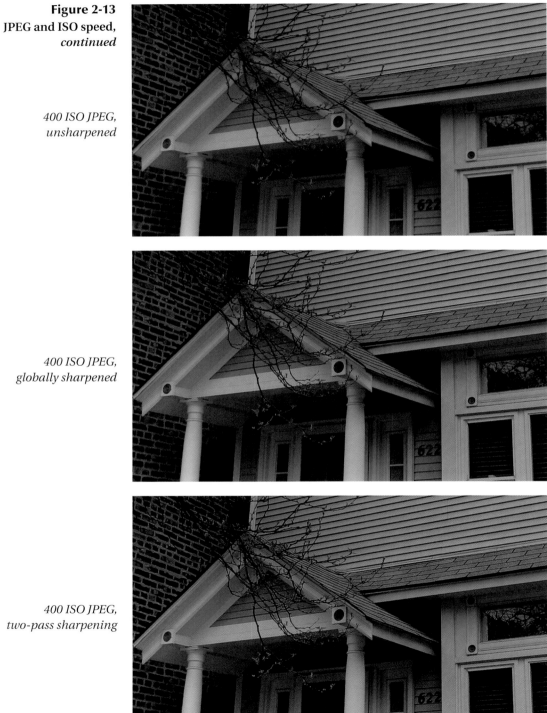

Figure 2-13
JPEG and ISO speed,
continued

*800 ISO JPEG,
unsharpened*

*800 ISO JPEG,
globally sharpened*

*800 ISO JPEG,
two-pass sharpening
with noise reduction*

Figure 2-13
JPEG and ISO speed,
continued

*1600 ISO JPEG,
unsharpened*

*1600 ISO JPEG,
globally sharpened*

*1600 ISO JPEG,
two-pass sharpening
with noise reduction*

At 100 ISO, the difference between global and two-pass sharpening is almost imperceptible, at least at this enlargement factor. But as ISO increases, the difference between the two approaches becomes more obvious, and it's clear that at 1600 ISO we need to apply noise reduction before sharpening to avoid obvious noise in both luminance and color.

Sharpening and the Image Source

For the past 30 pages, I've shown examples of different image source types, and their influence on sharpening, comparing traditional global sharpening with selective sharpening tailored to the image source. In some cases, the differences are obvious, while in others, they are extremely subtle. Rest assured that this was a conscious decision on my part!

What lessons can we draw from the preceding examples?

▶ The need to address the image source specifically is not clear-cut. In some cases, it may simply create extra work. In other cases, it's absolutely necessary if you want a usable image. Most real-world scenarios lie somewhere between these two extremes.

▶ The degree of enlargement is a key factor in determining the need for applying noise reduction and sharpening to the high-resolution data. I've shown you extremes— such as making a 19- by 27-inch print from a 35mm original, and making a 4.3- by 3-inch print from the same 35mm original. With greater enlargement, the need for sharpening tailored to the source becomes more likely. But the point at which it becomes necessary depends on both the source and the use.

▶ With larger film formats, or higher-resolution digital captures, the need to address grain and noise diminishes because the enlargement factor diminishes, unless, of course, you're pushing the limits to make the largest prints possible. In that case, you'll certainly get better results if you apply noise reduction and sharpening tailored specifically to the image source before doing final sharpening for output.

▶ ISO speed, whether on film or in digital captures, also plays a critical role. The higher the speed, the more noise, so for any given medium or any given use, specialized treatment will be required sooner at high ISO speeds than at lower ones.

▶ Underexposed digital images contain more noise, and hence are more likley to need special handling, than underexposed film images.

▶ The computer display can show you what is happening to the image pixels, but is a far-from-reliable guide to final printed appearance, because the size of the pixels on the display is typically much larger than the size of the pixels when translated to print.

▶ Understanding all of these factors is key not only in learning how to apply sharpening tailored to the image source, but also in deciding whether and when to do so.

Whie it's undoubtedly the most complex part of the whole equation, the image source is only one of the factors we need to understand and, in some cases, address when we sharpen. The next factor, and one which we *always* have to address in sharpening, is the image content.

Sharpening and Image Content

While the influence of the image source is subtle, the influence of the image content is quite obvious. In any given image, there exists a level of detail that we want to emphasize, but that level of detail varies from image to image. If we simply treat all images the same, we may end up either emphasizing unwanted detail or noise, or obscuring detail we really wanted to emphasize.

A "busy" image with lots of fine detail like the upper one in Figure 2-14 needs a much different treatment than one with soft detail like the lower one in Figure 2-14. Here they're shown with sharpening that takes the content into account.

Both images have received two passes of sharpening. The first pass matched the sharpening haloes to the size of the details we want to emphasize. The second pass was tailored to the 150-line halftone process. We'll look at the whole question of multipass sharpening in much more detail in Chapter 3, *Sharpening Strategies*, but for the moment, let's focus on the issue of matching sharpening radius to image content. The images in Figure 2-14 and the subsequent examples have all had identical sharpening applied in the second phase. The only difference is in the first sharpening pass.

Figure 2-14
Sharpening optimized
for image content

*Both of these images
have received two-pass
sharpening, with the
first pass matched to the
image content, and the
second pass matched to
the 150-lpi halftone
process used to print
this book.*

Content-Sensitive Sharpening

Figure 2-15 shows an extreme example of what can happen if we apply the wrong sharpening in the first pass. The top image has received the sharpening that was appropriate for the bottom image, and the bottom image has received the sharpening appropriate for the top one.

On the top image, applying the wrong sharpening produces an image that is lackluster. The wide sharpening haloes actually obscure some of the fine detail instead of making it more obvious, and the entire image seems soft—the opposite of the result we wanted!

On the bottom image, applying the wrong sharpening produces a more obviously unacceptable result. With an older model, the skin would look like a moonscape: 4-year-old Alice looks sandpapered because the incorrect sharpening has introduced unwanted texture by exaggerating the pattern from the camera mosaic itself.

A casual glance might lead us to conclude that the top image is undersharpened while the bottom image is oversharpened. In actuality, it's not the quantity of sharpening that's the problem, it's the *quality* of the sharpening. No matter how much we increased the intensity of the sharpening in the top image, we'd still wind up obscuring detail because the haloes are too wide, and if we backed off the amount of sharpening on the bottom image until the sandpaper disappeared, we'd have a soft, unsharpened image.

Low-Frequency and High-Frequency Images

The top image in Figures 2-14 and 2-15 is of the type known as a "high-frequency" image, because it has lots of sharp tonal transitions in a small area. The bottom image is of the type known as a "low-frequency" image because the tone stays relatively constant over a given small area and the tonal transitions are gradual rather than sudden.

Many if not most images contain both high-frequency and low-frequency components, but in the vast majority of cases, there's a single dominant tendency that we wish to emphasize. If you're willing to do a good deal of manual work, you can even sharpen low-frequency and high-frequency elements separately in a single image, but you can obtain good results with relatively little work by sharpening in the first pass for the dominant characteristics of the image.

To make the low-frequency/high-frequency distinction a little clearer, Figure 2-16 shows a single row of pixels from each image in Figure 2-14,

Figure 2-15
Incorrect sharpening
for image content

graphed according to their tonal values. The high-frequency image has sudden jumps in tonal value spread across a relatively small area, which is another way of saying that the image has lots of narrow edges. The low-frequency image features much more gradual transitions spread over a much wider area, indicating that the image contains big, wide edges.

When I applied the wide-edge sharpening to the high-frequency image in Figure 2-15, I created sharpening haloes that were much wider than the details in the image, so it ended up looking soft, and when I applied the narrow-edge sharpening to the low-frequency image in Figure 2-15, I emphasized the small tonal transitions that represented texture rather than edges, producing the sandpaper effect.

Figure 2-16
High-frequency and
low-frequency images

*A high-frequency
image has many strong
tonal transitions in a
small area.*

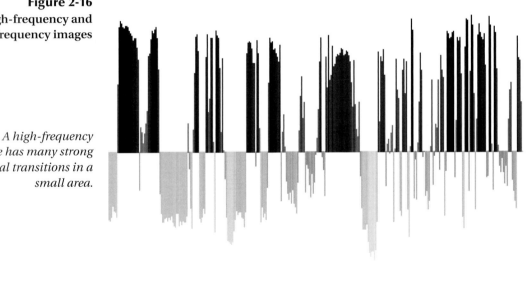

*A low-frequency image
has smooth tonal
transitions spread
across a large area.*

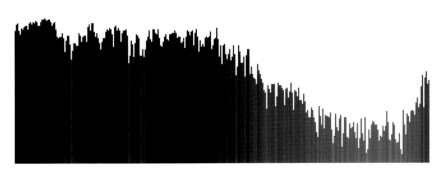

As I noted earlier, it's easy to mistake the wrong *kind* of sharpening for the wrong amount of sharpening. I'll discuss the tools and techniques that let us influence both the quality and the quantity of sharpening in much more detail in Chapter 4, *Sharpening Tools and Techniques*, but for now let's stay focused on the sharpening requirements themselves rather than how to obtain them.

At the beginning of this chapter, I emphasized the difficulty of using the monitor as a guide for print sharpening. Figure 2-17 shows sections of the images from Figure 2-14 printed at approximately the resolution of the display. They look quite ugly, but these are exactly the same pixels used to print Figure 2-14.

Figure 2-17
Sharpened pixels

A magnified view of the pixels used to print the images in Figure 2-14, that corresponds approximately to the view you'd see if you looked at the images on the computer display at Actual Pixels (100%) zoom factor.

Detail of the images from Figure 2-14 at Actual Pixels view

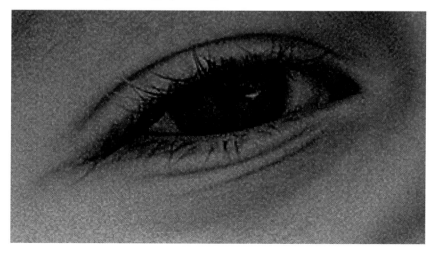

The magnified pixels look fairly hideous, especially in the upper, high-frequency image, but when they're rendered in print, the objectionable "jaggies" are simply too small for the eye to pick them out as distinct features. Instead, we see a sharp image.

What the computer display does show is the difference in the sharpening haloes between the high-frequency and low-frequency images. The high-frequency image has very small, high-contrast haloes, while the low-frequency image has larger, lower-contrast ones. Ultimately, you have to gain experience with your own display at judging sharpening, but the one factor you always need to bear in mind is the size of the pixels on final output. Faced with scary-looking images on screen, many of us end up undersharpening our images.

How Sharp Is Sharp Enough?

Figure 2-18 shows different sharpening treatments of the same image, ranging from unsharpend to oversharpened. To some degree, sharpening

Figure 2-18   How sharp is sharp enough?

The image with no sharpening

*The image with a single pass of sharpening tailored
for the output process*

is a matter of taste, but I suspect that most readers will agree that the image at the extreme left in Figure 2-18 is undersharpened (in fact, it isn't sharpened at all), and the one at the extreme right is oversharpened.

The difference between the two middle images is more subtle (but again, subtle differences are ultimately what this book is all about). My own opinion is that the image sharpened in two passes (the third from the left) has more of an illusion of "depth" than the one sharpened with a single pass (second from the left). The peeling bark has more texture, though not overly so, and the background foliage is more clearly defined. The highlights are a little less bright, and contain more detail.

Now let's look at the actual pixels—you may find them surprising!

Figure 2-18   How sharp is sharp enough?

The image with multipass sharpening for both content and output

The image with typical one-pass oversharpening

The image in Figure 2-19 with no sharpening, at the extreme left, looks soft at Actual Pixels view, and it's no suprise that it also prints that way, though it doesn't look as soft at the reduced print size in Figure 2-18 as it does at Actual Pixels view.

The image sharpened with a single pass for output, second from the left, looks reasonably sharp at Actual Pixels view, but still prints a little soft. It's acceptable, but it's less sharp than it could be.

The image sharpened with multiple passes looks downright crunchy at Actual Pixels view, yet it prints well. Note that while the edges appear jagged, the highlights and shadows still hold detail, and the sharpening contours, while strong, are relatively narrow, so they don't obscure any fine details. In short, the sharpening is matched to the image content.

Figure 2-19   Sharpening and pixels

The image with no sharpening   *The image with a single pass of sharpening tailored for the output process*

The final image, at right, is indeed oversharpened—lots of pixels have been forced to pure white or solid black. But the underlying problem is that the sharpening haloes are too big, obscuring detail rather than emphasizing it. The combination of over-large haloes and too much sharpening also causes some hue shifts, such as the bright lime greens in the upper-left corner that aren't present in any of the other versions.

In the real world, this is often what happens when a client looks at a proof and asks for "more sharpening." What they really need is a different *kind* of sharpening that is sensitive to the image content, but when they ask for more sharpening, that's exactly what they get, so highlights get blown to white and shadows get plugged to black, without actually fixing the problem.

Figure 2-19   Sharpening and pixels

The image with multipass sharpening for both content and output   *The image with typical one-pass oversharpening*

Taking Sharpening to the Limit

The main argument that is raised against sharpening images more than once is that you'll end up with an oversharpened mess. It's certainly possible to destroy images with multiple rounds of sharpening, but as you just saw in Figure 2-18 and 2-19, it's equally possible to do so with just one ill-considered sharpening pass.

I'll discuss the basic philosophy behinds multipass sharpening in Chapter 3, *Sharpening Strategies,* and provide detailed recipes for the various phases of sharpening in Chapter 5, *Putting the Tools to Work,* but this chapter is all about results, so let's look at a couple of examples that show just how far you can push sharpening without breaking the image.

Figure 2-20 shows four versions of the same image, ranging from the unsharpened version at the extreme left, through a one-pass sharpened

Figure 2-20   How sharp can you get?

Not sharp   *Sharp*

version second from left, a two-pass sharpened version third from the left, to a multipass sharpened version at the extreme right.

Again, the differences are subtle, but they're there if you look. The unsharpened version is, of course, soft. The one-pass sharpening produces acceptable results, but doesn't come close to revealing all the detail that's available.

The two-pass sharpening does a substantially better job—we start to see the scratches on the polished metal—but the basket of ivy in the lower-right corner is still a little soft. The version at the extreme right has some extra sharpening applied in specific areas (such as the ivy basket) as well as the two rounds of global sharpening it shares with the previous image. In all, this version has actually had four separate sharpening routines applied, two globally, two locally, yet it looks sharp rather than crunchy.

Figure 2-20   How sharp can you get?

Sharper   *Sharpest*

The relationship between pixels on the computer display and final print dots is sufficiently indirect that we can't really judge final output sharpness from the display without a good deal of experience: But looking at the pixels on the display is one of the essential paths to gaining that experience. The key point to remember is that optimally sharpened images often look ugly on screen, particularly at higher zoom levels.

Figure 2-21 shows a detail from the images in Figure 2-20 at approximately 300% zoom factor. Until you know how to interpret the 300% view, it may well scare you, but unless you develop the habit of looking at the pixels and drawing correlations between them and the printed result, you'll never learn how to interpret the on-screen appearance.

At 300% view, the individual pixels are clearly visible, and you can see exactly what happens to them as you sharpen. Remember, though, that

Figure 2-21   Pixels at 300% zoom

Not sharp   *Sharp*

these images are sharpened for the 150-line halftone screen used throughout this book, at a resolution of 300 ppi. If the pixels were reproduced exactly, each one would be only 0.03 inches wide, which is well below the threshold of human visual acuity, but at 300 ppi, it actually takes four image pixels to make a single halftone dot.

We can't control the halftoning process, and unless you're unusually knowledgable about screening algorithms, it's just about impossible to know which four pixels will go to make up a particular cyan, magenta, yellow, or black dot on the print. What you *can* do is to examine the sharpening haloes, and check that they aren't too wide. If you examine Figure 2-21 carefully, you'll see that while the contrast along edges increases from the left image to the right one, the size of the sharpening haloes remains at a constant two to three pixels wide. This is wide enough to provide the

Figure 2-21   Pixels at 300% zoom

Sharper   *Sharpest*

appearance of sharpness in the print, but is still too small for the eye to pick out the halo as a discrete feature. We get the benefit of the sharpening haloes without making them obvious in the print, which is the key to good sharpening.

Which leads us to the last of the three factors we need to address when we sharpen—the softening introduced by the output process.

Sharpening and the Output Process

Just as the process of turning photons into pixels introduces softness, so does the process of turning pixels into marks on a substrate (typically but not always ink on paper). There are three basic types of printed output.

▶ **Halftone** output (see Figure 2-22), used on most printing presses and some color laser printers, turns the pixels into regularly spaced variable-sized dots. The spacing between the dots is called the *screen frequency*, and is usually expressed in lines per inch. Light tones are produced by small dots, dark tones by larger ones.

This book is printed using a 150-line-per-inch screen. Trade magazines typically use 133 lines per inch, newspapers use 85 lines per inch or, on modern presses, up to 120 lines per inch. Glossy magazine covers and premium-quality print jobs use 175 lines per inch, and some fine art coffee-table books may use 200 or even 300 lines per inch, though the latter is still very rare.

▶ **Error diffusion dither** output (see Figure 2-22), used on almost all ink-jet printers, many color laser printers, and on a few printing presses (where it's more commonly known as stochastic screening), turns the pixels into fixed-sized dots with variable placement. Light tones are produced by printing fewer dots in a given area, dark tones are produced by printing more dots in that same area.

Some inkjet printers offer "variable-size dots." Don't confuse these with halftone dots, which are *continuously* variable in size—the inkjets that use this feature typically have only two dot sizes, the larger one being used only in dark areas.

Figure 2-22
Halftones and
diffusion dithers

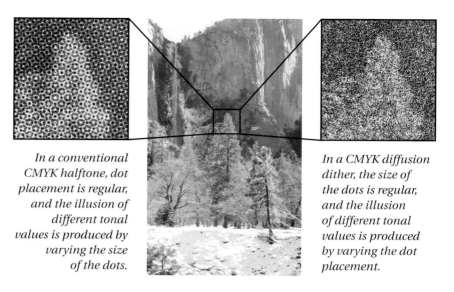

*In a conventional
CMYK halftone, dot
placement is regular,
and the illusion of
different tonal
values is produced by
varying the size
of the dots.*

*In a CMYK diffusion
dither, the size of
the dots is regular,
and the illusion
of different tonal
values is produced
by varying the dot
placement.*

▶ **Continuous-tone** output includes dye-sublimation printers, and print-ers such as the Fuji Pictrography and Frontier, the Océ LightJet, and the Durst Lambda, which use color lasers to expose traditional photo-graphic paper. Unlike the first two technologies under discussion, this type of printer prints dots that have the same properties as pixels—the dots are all the same size, and all three (cyan, magenta, and yellow) colors are laid down in the same dot, varying density of each color to produce different tone and color values.

With continuous-tone printers, the relationship between image pixels and print dots is direct—one pixel in the image produces one dot on the print—but the dots are round where the image pixels are square, and the edges are softer than pixels displayed on an LCD (though prob-ably not on a CRT) display. However, unless you're printing an unusu-ally low-resolution image, the print dots are likely to be much smaller than the image pixels viewed on the display.

We can't control the way pixels get turned into dots. What we *can* control is the resolution—the number of pixels per inch—we send to the print device, and the way we sharpen those pixels. Moreover, the resolutions we usually send to the various different print technologies aren't just picked out of thin air. They're based on the physiology of the eye itself, which imposes limits on the finest detail we can see.

Resolution and the Eye

It should be obvious, but I'll state it anyway, that it takes two photore-ceptors to detect a difference in luminance or color, because to detect a difference, you need two signals. It follows that the smallest difference we could possibly see is one that is projected onto two photoreceptors on the retina.

Human visual acuity. The generally accepted definition of normal (20/20) visual acuity is the ability to resolve a spatial pattern whose features are separated by one minute of arc, or 1/60 of a degree. This number comes directly from the retina. The lens in the eye projects one degree of the scene across 288 micrometers (or microns) of the retina.

In the area of the retina where the photoreceptors are most tightly packed, the fovea, a linear 288 micrometers contains about 120 photore-ceptors. So, if more than 120 alternating black and white lines, or 60 cycles, are projected onto this area, someone with normal visual acuity will see a solid gray mass. Most printing processes exploit this fact to create the illusions of continuous tone from a bunch of discrete dots.

The actual size of the features that fall at the limit of visual acuity de-pend, of course, on viewing distance. With a little trigonometry, we can calculate the threshold of normal visual acuity for a given viewing distance. One minute of arc (1/60 of a degree) is 0.00029089 radians. We can calcu-late the limit L of visual acuity at distance D by the formula:

$L=D*TAN(0.00029089)$

Table 2-2 shows the limit of visual acuity at different viewing distances, and the minimum print resolution, in dots per inch, needed to provide the illusion of continuous tone to an observer with 20/20 vision.

	Viewing Distance (inches)	Limit (inches)	PPI
Table 2-2			
Viewing distance	8	0.00232	428
and resolution	12	0.00349	286
	15	0.00436	229
	18	0.00524	191
	20	0.00582	172
	24	0.00698	143

However, these numbers, although useful, aren't set in stone for the following important reasons.

▶ Most of the work done to establish these limits uses black and white line pairs, but our ability to discern individual features diminishes as contrast is reduced, so in most real imagery (which is *not* comprised of black and white line pairs) the practical limit may be larger and hence the required ppi to provide the illusion of continuous tone may be lower.

▶ Conversely, some people have better than 20/20 vision. The maximum acuity of the unaided human eye is generally thought to be about 20/15 (meaning that the observer can distinguish details at 20 feet that some-one with "normal" 20/20 vision could only distinguish at 15 feet), and with modern corrective lenses, 20/10 vision (where the observer can distinguish details at 20 feet that someone with "normal" 20/20 vision could only distinguish at 10 feet) may be achievable.

▶ A slew of other factors can come into play, including but not limited to defects in the eye's lens, the pupil size, the level of illumination, the duration of exposure to the target, the area of the retina that is stimu-lated, the state of adaptation of the eye, and eye movement.

So treat the numbers in Table 2-2 as useful guidelines rather than as absolutes. One reason for mentioning these numbers is to provide insight into the reasons we print at the resolutions we typically use, but another equally important reason is to help us understand what we need to do to keep our sharpening haloes near the threshold of visual acuity. By doing so, we can produce prints that appear sharp, yet lack the obvious and disturb-ing sharpening haloes that mar so much of the work we see in print.

Viewing distance. I've observed the phenomenon so many times that I can't resist commenting on it. When some otherwise-sane photographers learn that a print was produced digitally, the concept of "normal viewing distance" suddenly changes from the distance at which they can see the image to one that is largely determined by the length of their noses. If you examine a 30- by 40-inch traditional darkroom print at that distance, you'll likely see grain artifacts that become invisible when you move back far enough to see the image. It's the same with digital!

Figure 2-23 contains 75 line pairs per inch, with increasing contrast from solid midtone gray at the top to solid black and white at the bottom. As you move the image further or closer to your eye, the point at which you can no longer discern the individual line pairs changes. As you move closer, you can discern the line pairs higher up the page, and if you move back far enough, the whole figure becomes one solid gray mass.

Notice that the right side of the figure is different from the left side. The difference is that the left side of the figure has had no sharpening applied, while the right side has been sharpened. As a result, you can discern the line pairs on the right side higher up than you can do so on the left side at any given viewing distance.

This is exactly what good sharpening does. It increases localized contrast to reveal detail. But each printing process imposes its own requirements and limitations.

Print Resolution

When we print, we need to decide how many pixels per inch we send to the printing process. In part, the decision depends on how many pixels we captured in the first place. We can create more pixels by interpolation, but interpolation can't create detail—it simply takes the original pixels, spreads them apart, and creates new pixels with intermediate values in the spaces between the original ones.

When interpolation is combined with careful sharpening, it can improve the print results very slightly on some images, but it tends to be a great deal of extra work for questionable return. I recommend attempting only when printing at the uninterpolated resolution has clearly failed.

Interpolating downward to achieve the required output resolution is, however, necessary and normal. It's possible to drown printers in data: If you send far more data than the printer can resolve, it will either throw the excess data away (in which case you've just wasted some time), or, worse, it will attempt to use the extra data, with the result that detail gets blocked up instead of being resolved.

In either case, final sharpening for print *must* be done after any interpolation. If you downsample, the sharpening haloes can simply disappear as they're downsampled out of existence, and if you upsample, the sharpening haloes become too large and hence visually obvious. The print sharpening must always be done at the final print resolution.

Figure 2-23
Line pairs with
increasing contrast

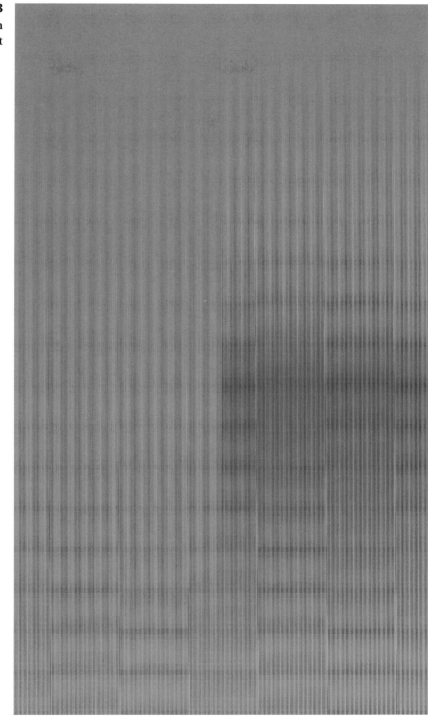

Halftone output. The general rule of thumb for halftone output is to send a number of pixels per inch that corresponds to between 1.5 and 2 times the screen frequency in lines per inch. If the platesetter or the imagesetter is driven by PostScript (which they invariably are), anything over 2.5 times the screen frequency is automatically discarded, so it's an absolute certainty that there's no reason to send more than 2.5 times the screen frequency.

In the real world, I've yet to encounter an image that showed any visible difference when printed from 2.5 the screen frequency instead of 2 times the screen frequency. But images with fine detail generally reproduce better when 2 times the screen frequency is used rather than 1.5 times the screen frequency, particularly at lower screen rulings. At higher screen frequencies of 175 lpi and greater, the difference becomes more subtle and is apparent on fewer images.

Figure 2-24 shows the same image printed from a 300 ppi file (native resolution, 2x the screen frequency) and from a 225 ppi file (downsampled from 300 to 225 ppi, 1.5x the screen frequency). Can you see the difference? (There *are* differences—I had to sharpen the 225 ppi version more aggressively for output than I did the 300 ppi version—but they're quite subtle!)

Continuous-tone output. A great deal depends on the software used to drive the continuous-tone printer, but a useful rule of thumb is to send pixels at the printer's native resolution. Some older dye-sublimation printers may still insist that you do so, but most modern continuous-tone printers have sophisticated controllers that will perform the necessary interpolation to the printer's native resolution.

Some advocate sticking to resolutions that are even multiples of the printer's native resolution. Doing so certainly simplifies the interpolation tasks that the software controller needs to conduct, but I've only found the practice to be advantageous with some older printers and with some entry-level dye-sub printers.

It's almost certainly a bad idea to send significantly *more* than the printer's native resolution, not because the interpolation algorithms will do a bad job, but simply because in doing you lose some control over the sharpening since the sharpening haloes will be downsampled along with the rest of the image. But it's not worth downsampling an image that had been prepared at 305 ppi for a Fuji Frontier to 300 ppi before printing it on

Figure 2-24
Resolution for halftone

This image had one pass of sharpening applied before downsampling to 300 ppi, and one pass of sharpening for print.

This image had the same one pass of sharpening applied before downsampling to 225 ppi, and one pass of sharpening for print.

a 300 ppi Océ LightJet—the difference is just too small to worry about on normal images. (You may see a detectable difference on synthetic targets made up of black and white line pairs, but that difference disappears with even slightly lowered contrast.) Most minilabs and online services who offer continuous-tone output specify 300 ppi for high-quality printing. If you aren't sure about the optimal ppi for your preferred service, ask!

Error diffusion dither output. Most inkjet and color laser printers use an error diffusion dither of some kind, though the details are usually proprietary. Most color laser printers quote a resolution of 600 or 1200 dots per inch, while most inkjet printers specify some multiple of these resolutions. Canon's photo inkjet printers range from 1200 x 1200 dpi to 9600 x 2400 dpi, Hewlett-Packard's photo inkjets generally use 4800 x 1200 dpi, while Epson's inkjet printers typically specify 720 x 2880 or 1440 x 5760 dpi.

What these numbers represent is the *addressable* resolution of the printer—the accuracy with which it attempts to lay down dots of ink. Their relationship to the pixel resolution of the image is fairly indirect, but the optimal ppi value is lower than these numbers may suggest. The conventional wisdom is that the "native" resolution of Epson inkjets is 360 ppi, while that of the Canon and Hewlett-Packard inkjets is 300 ppi.

What my own testing indicates is that there's definitely no point in upsampling images to achieve a resolution higher than the native ones stated above, and little point in upsampling even to these resolutions. For large prints that are likely to be viewed from 20 inches or more, 180 ppi is probably plenty.

However, if you're making small prints, and you have real captured data (that is, with no interpolation) in excess of the native resolution, you may not want to downsample it to the native resolution. With Epson printers, there seems to be a small but useful advantage to sending 480 ppi of real data, *suitably sharpened*, to the printer. At higher resolutions the advantage diminishes, and sending more than 720 ppi actually seems to degrade the image.

Some pundits claim that you'll always get better results if you print at even multiples of the native resolution. This holds true for line pair targets, but on real-world images the benefit is much less certain, and may often be outweighed by the damage done by resampling the image. I almost always print at the native capture resolution, and if that turns out to be 342 ppi rather than 360, or 191 ppi rather than 180, I simply don't worry about it.

Note, however, that this is simply a statement of what I do, albeit based on considerable testing and experience. Each generation of new printers brings new capabilities and, probably, new challenges, so beware of any statements on optimal resolution for inkjet printers that claim to be definitive, and don't be afraid to put conventional wisdom to the test!

Sharpening for Output

Whether you adopt the multipass workflow I'll advocate in Chapter 3, *Sharpening Strategies*, or the more traditional single-pass sharpening, output sharpening is where the strongest sharpening comes into play. The key point to bear in mind when sharpening for output is that it's resolution dependent—it's all about the size of the pixels.

Remember—you have no control over how the pixels get turned into dots, so all you can do is to sharpen the pixels themselves. So for any given size of output, you need to sharpen higher-resolution images more aggressively than lower-resolution ones to achieve the same perceived sharpness. More aggressive sharpening can mean wider haloes, higher contrast between dark and light contours, or a combination of both.

The goal with output sharpening is produce a satisfactorily sharp image without introducing visually obvious sharpening haloes. To do so, the secret is to keep the size of the haloes below the threshold of visual acuity at the anticipated viewing distance—this is where the size of the pixels on output becomes a critical factor.

Bear in mind that the numbers given in Table 2-2 for the limits of visual acuity refer to very high-contrast edges indeed, since they're based on black and white line pairs. In practice, you can take some liberties with these numbers. The following rules of thumb have served me well.

▶ For smaller size reproductions, such as small inkjet prints, magazine reproduction, or most of the images in this book, I try to keep the light and dark sharpening haloes to around 0.01 inches each. If I'm printing to an inkjet printer at 360 ppi, that means that the sharpening haloes can be as wide as 3.6 pixels if the image content requires it, and if I'm printing a 200 ppi image to a 133-line halftone, I need to keep the haloes to around 1 pixel for the light halo and one pixel for the dark one.

▶ For larger reproductions, I may relax these limits to make light and dark contours of around 0.02 inches. If I'm making a large inkjet print at 180 ppi, which is the lowest resolution I typically print, that still allows light and dark haloes of close to 2 pixels each. However, I still try to keep the haloes as small as possible, varying the contrast to make the contours stronger or weaker.

Paper stock also has an influence. Inks bleed more on uncoated papers than on coated ones, so sharpening for uncoated papers has to be stronger than that for coated papers to achieve the same degree of sharpness.

Figure 2-25 shows the same native-resolution pixels sharpened for different print sizes and processes, zoomed in to approximately 400% view to make the differences obvious. The sharpening for the 4 by 6 inkjet print appears the gentlest of the three, because the inkjet can actually resolve the fine detail that wider sharpening haloes would obscure.

Figure 2-25
Size-sensitive sharpening

This is the entire image, downsampled to 300 ppi for this reproduction. The area of interest that we'll examine is outlined in black.

Detail of the above image at capture resolution, sharpened for a 6- by 4-inch inkjet print at 480 ppi

The haloes for the halftone sharpening are wider than for the inkjet, because it takes several pixels to make up one halftone dot. Hence rendering single-pixel details isn't possible (you could render single-pixel details by sending a lower-resolution image, but then you'd have obvious single pixels, which looks worse than bad sharpening). The haloes for the 85-line halftone need to be higher-contrast than those for the 175-line halftone to achieve the same apparent sharpness.

Figure 2-25
Size-sensitive sharpening,
continued

*Detail of the image
at capture resolution,
sharpened for a 20- by
14-inch 85-line halftone
print at 127 ppi
(1.5 x line screen)*

*Detail of the image
at capture resolution,
sharpened for a 7.75- by
5-inch 175-line halftone
print at 350 ppi*

There's one last thing to note about output sharpening. Unlike the other sharpening factors I've discussed, the relationship between pixels and printer dots, for any given print process at any given resolution, is fixed, and doesn't depend on image content or source. I'll discuss the implications of this in detail in the next chapter, *Sharpening Strategies*.

Creative Sharpening

There's one more reason we sharpen, which is to tell the story we want to tell, and that often involves improving reality. The concept of improving reality is anathema to some photographers, and if you're one of them, feel free to skip this section, but do recognize that it's what some other photographers get paid to do!

We sometimes want to call extra attention to an element in an image by making it appear a little sharper than its surroundings. Head shots often benefit from a little extra sharpening around the eyes, for example. I call this kind of sharpening "creative sharpening" because unlike the other kinds of sharpening I've discussed so far—source-sensitive, content-sensitive, and output-sensitive sharpening—creative sharpening can't be automated. It requires manual application and human decision making.

Figure 2-26 shows two images before creative sharpening on the left, and after creative sharpening on the right. On the top image, I added a little extra sharpening to the eyes and hair. On the bottom image, I added extra sharpening to the wall to reveal the cracks and texture, but not to the doors or the ground.

There are really no hard and fast rules, beyond those imposed by good taste, regarding creative sharpening. Obviously, if you overdo it, you'll wind up with a crunchy image, and if you don't do it enough you'll waste time doing things that don't show up in the final image, but within those bounds you have a lot of leeway.

A reasonable rule of thumb is to apply creative sharpening in such a way that it doesn't stick out from the rest of the image as an area that has obviously been more heavily sharpened—the transition between the areas that have received creative sharpening and those that have not should be imperceptible at Actual Pixels (100%) zoom or lower. The smoothness of the transition is more important than the actual appearance of the pixels on the screen unless you're actually sharpening for on-screen viewing.

Figure 2-26   Creative sharpening

One Size Does Not Fit All

This chapter contains a lot of details, but the overall message is that, when it comes to sharpening, one size doesn't fit all. If you fail to take the image source into account, you end up sharpening noise as well as detail. If you ignore the image content, you may exaggerate unwanted detail, or obscure wanted detail. And if you don't tailor the sharpening for the output process, your images will appear undersharpened or oversharpened.

The challenge, then, is to reconcile these disparate needs to produce optimally sharpened images. In the next chapter, *Sharpening Strategies*, I'll discuss a sharpening workflow that attempts to do just that.

3

Sharpening Strategies

Building a Sharpening Workflow

In the last chapter, we saw that sharpening has to take into account several different and often contradictory demands. In this chapter, I'll offer a means of reconciling these disparate demands, while pointing out the potential pitfalls in doing so.

Having tried for decades to meet all the requirements imposed by image source, image content, and image use in a single sharpening operation, I've reluctantly concluded that it is in fact impossible to do so. Of course, this conclusion flies in the face of conventional wisdom, which dictates that sharpening should be applied in a single pass as either the last or next-to-last step (before conversion to final CMYK in an RGB workflow) in the image reproduction chain. But the conventional wisdom does have some foundation.

- ▶ Back when the drum scanner was king, images were usually scanned directly to CMYK, at reproduction size, with sharpening applied by the scanner. The conventional wisdom workflow tries to replicate this.

- ▶ If downsampling is done after sharpening, the image has to be resharpened, because the haloes get downsampled out of existence.

- ▶ Multiple passes of sharpening tend to ruin images.

These are all good points that deserve careful consideration, but let's look at the downsides to the conventional wisdom.

Traditional Prepress Sharpening

First, let's be clear that traditional sharpening works reasonably well as long as it's done with the requisite skill and the built-in assumptions aren't violated. But there's a substantial difference between "reasonably well" and "optimally."

In the traditional sharpening workflow, sharpening is applied either as the final process (which allows tricks like sharpening only the black plate, so that eyelashes and hair get sharpened, but skin textures don't), or as the next-to-last process before conversion to final CMYK. It offers a simple workflow (which is no small advantage), but it also has its share of disadvantages.

One-Pass Sharpening Is Inflexible

A key assumption in the traditional sharpening workflow is that the final use is known, and the image has been sized for that final use. Back in the rubylith days, this assumption was generally valid, but as soon as page layout applications gave designers the ability to resize images in the layout, that assumption went out the window.

Nowadays, it's common practice for prepress operations to act both as suppliers of original scans, and as the final step in the output chain. As a result, it's not uncommon for scanned images to receive two rounds of sharpening, once at the time of the scan on the high-resolution image, then again on the resized image before output. The key point is that traditional sharpening is designed to be applied to the final image at final output resolution, and the further the image is from that state, the less successful the sharpening is likely to be.

Tip: Buy Unsharpened Scans. If you're buying drum scans for images whose final use is unknown, or you're buying drum scans to use as master images for multiple outputs, specify no sharpening during the scan process. Inappropriate sharpening is extremely hard to undo, and unless the images are scanned to their final output resolution, any sharpening applied during the scan is almost guaranteed to be inappropriate. Even if you opt to stay with a one-pass sharpening workflow, that workflow will work better when you reserve sharpening for the final output-sized image.

One-Pass Sharpening Is Often Overdone

Since traditional sharpening, as it is commonly use today, is sensitive neither to image content nor to final use, it's common to see grossly oversharpened images, especially in the case where a sharpened scan receives a second round of sharpening at final output size.

Figure 3-1 shows an image scanned without sharpening, then sharpened carefully in two passes, and the same image sharpened during the scan, then again after resizing.

Figure 3-1
Oversharpening

This version of the image was scanned with no sharpening, then sharpened carefully in two passes, once on the high-resolution scan, then again at final output resolution.

This version of the image was sharpened during the scan, then sharpened again at final output size, using "standard" sharpening techniques.

While this kind of oversharpening is rare in high-end work (because someone has paid to make sure that it doesn't happen), it's depressingly commonplace in commercial publishing. However, this is not an argument against multi-pass sharpening: Both versions of the image in Figure 3-1 received two sharpening passes. Rather, it's an argument against careless sharpening that fails to account for image content and final use.

One-Pass Sharpening and Digital Capture

Traditional one-pass sharpening is very much tailored to scanned transparencies, since it essentially simulates the sharpening built into drum scanners. (It's possible to get good drum scans from color negative, but relatively few operators know how to do so.)

Traditional sharpening is global. A salient feature of traditional sharpening is that it's applied globally to the entire image. While this worked reasonably well with transparency scans, it generally fails to do justice to digital raw captures, where it sharpens the noise along with the edges.

The problem becomes worse when global sharpening is also applied by the conversion software that translates the raw camera capture into a rendered RGB image. (Bear in mind that when you shoot JPEG, the camera itself performs a raw conversion, often with sharpening applied as default.) Figure 3-2 shows a range of possibilities from a digital raw capture.

Figure 3-2
Digital raw capture

This version of the image was produced by applying traditional one-pass sharpening at print size to an unsharpened raw image. As a result, it's undersharpened.

Most raw converters offer the option to produce an unsharpened image, but many photographers decline to exercise this option because the results are obviously soft on the display. Yet many of the major stock agencies specify that submissions should be unsharpened. This is a recipe for soft images.

Global sharpening in the raw converter followed by traditional sharpening produces images with sharp noise, but not necessarily with sharp detail. The two-pass sharpening used on the image at the bottom of this page accounts for image source and content, producing the best result.

Figure 3-2
Digital raw capture,
continued

This version of the image was produced by applying global sharpening in the raw converter, followed by traditional one-pass sharpening at print size. The noise is sharp, but the detail is not.

This version of the image was produced by applying selective sharpening at high resolution, followed by output sharpening at print size. It's the best rendering of the three.

Traditional sharpening fails to exploit digital capture. By its nature, digital capture, unsharpened, produces images that both tolerate and require a good deal more sharpening than those from film. Most digital cameras actually include an optical low-pass filter to prevent color artifacting, which has the effect of softening the image. As a result, traditional sharpening, which is optimized for transparency scans, often undersharpens digital captures. Figure 3-3 shows the difference between a traditionally sharpened and an optimally sharpened digital raw capture.

Figure 3-3
Digital raw capture and
undersharpening

This version of the image was produced by applying global sharpening in the raw converter, followed by traditional one-pass sharpening at print size. It's not as sharp as it could be.

This version of the image was produced by applying selective sharpening at high resolution, followed by output sharpening at print size. It's noticably sharper than the version above.

This failure to understand the inherent properties of digital capture and the differences between digital capture and scanned transparencies has given rise to a considerable body of prepress myth regarding the perceived superiority of film over digital capture. But like it or not, digital capture has already largely replaced film for most commercial work, and the trend is clear and irreversible.

Traditional Sharpening Roots

Traditional sharpening is rooted in the drum scanner, and, moreover, in the analog drum scanner. The earliest drum scanners, from the 1960s, were analog devices that produced actual CMYK film separations, and the sharpening was done optically. By the 1980s, drum scanners produced digital CMYK files, still with optical sharpening.

When the desktop revolution hit in the early 1990s, the old paradigm of scanning at final resolution for a specific use fell by the wayside. Photoshop 2.0 introduced CMYK support, and changed print manufacturing forever, though not overnight—proprietary systems from the likes of Scitex, Linotype-Hell, Crosfield, and Agfa continued to hold sway for much of the decade, but by 1999, Photoshop had become not only a ubiquitous noun, but also a verb.

Photoshop sharpening practice. As has often been the case when an analog process is replaced by a digital one, most practitioners of sharpening in Photoshop used Photoshop's sharpening tools to replicate the drum scanning workflow. There is still considerable debate as to whether to sharpen before or after conversion to CMYK (some even advocate converting to Lab and sharpening the Lightness channel), but it's generally agreed that sharpening must be done at the final output size and resolution, after all major tonal adjustments have already been performed.

Traditional sharpening problems. The main problem with the traditional sharpening approach is that it tries to account for image source, image content, and output process in a single round of sharpening. After 15 years of experience using Photoshop to produce images both on press and on desktop printers, I concluded that it's simply impossible to address all three factors in one sharpening pass. The preceding pages of this book show the kinds of problems that arise when we attempt to do so. While the results aren't invariably bad, they're never as good as they could be.

Multipass sharpening problems. Many Photoshop users have at some point tried a multipass sharpening approach. A few have made it work, but the vast majority have wound up creating grossly oversharpened images, usually by falling into one or more of three potential pitfalls.

▶ Relying on the computer display to judge sharpness is a practice fraught with peril, yet until we make the print, it's all we have. The temptation is to make the image look sharp on screen, then to sharpen it again for output, often with unacceptable results.

▶ Failure to take image content into account in the first round of sharpening typically results in applying the wrong *kind* of sharpening for the image, so wanted detail may be obscured and unwanted detail or noise may be exaggerated.

▶ Applying the first pass of sharpening globally rather than through a mask that isolates edges sharpens noise and flat textured areas such as skies as well as sharpening the edges. When the second pass of sharpening is applied, the image becomes oversharpened.

▶ Applying the first pass of sharpening to the entire tonal range, rather than protecting the extreme highlights and shadows, almost guarantees that the second pass of sharpening will create blown highlights and plugged shadows.

The good news is that all of these problems are avoidable given sufficient attention, care, and skill. Building a multipass sharpening workflow is not a trivial undertaking, but neither is it impossible—otherwise I wouldn't have bothered writing this book!

A Multipass Sharpening Workflow

It's impossible to address the varying needs of the image source, the image content, and the output process in a single pass, because each imposes requirements that can contradict the others. The solution, then, is to build a multipass sharpening workflow that addresses the individual needs separately.

Each component has its own requirements, and by ignoring everything else, we can tailor each sharpening pass to address a specific issue.

Optimizing for the Image Source

Optimization for the image source is dictated by two factors—the noise signature, and the amount of detail the system can record. The goal of the first pass is to create an image that responds well to subsequent rounds of sharpening aimed at the image content, and at the output process. I recommend performing any major tonal correction before doing any sharpening or noise reduction, because major tonal manipulations can easily undo the sharpening or noise reduction if it's done beforehand.

The inherent softness of most digital captures (due to the antialiasing filter) requires actual sharpening, where with film the emphasis may be on grain reduction instead.

Optimizing digital captures. With digital capture, the lens is more often than not the practical limiting factor on the amount of detail the system can record, but the optical low-pass (antialiasing) filter found in the majority of digital SLRs sets an absolute limit.

For those few cameras that lack an antialiasing filter, it may be worthwhile making lens-specific settings, but in general we can come up with a single sharpening routine that is optimal for a given camera. High-ISO shots and significantly underexposed images may need special handling of noise, in either the raw converter or in Photoshop. Severe noise may call for a dedicated third-party noise reduction plug-in.

With normal exposures at low ISO settings, it's often enough to simply avoid sharpening the noise by protecting the extreme shadows. Any special noise reduction should always be applied before any sharpening!

Optimizing film captures. It's a little more difficult to make generalizations about film capture since the scanner represents a huge variable in both tonal rendering and resolution. With film, the amount of resolvable detail may be limited by the film grain or by the lens. On most film captures, the first pass is less about sharpening the image and more about mitigating the film grain. At one extreme, 35mm color negative requires strong grain reduction, while at the other extreme, large-format (4 x 5 or 8 x 10) transparencies can usually skip the first pass altogether.

Practical source optimization. Figure 3-4 shows three views of a well-exposed digital capture before and after treatment for the image source.

Figure 3-4
Source optimization for a
digital raw capture

The entire image,
downsampled to print
size, unsharpened

Unsharpened image
detail at "contact print"
(300 ppi) resolution

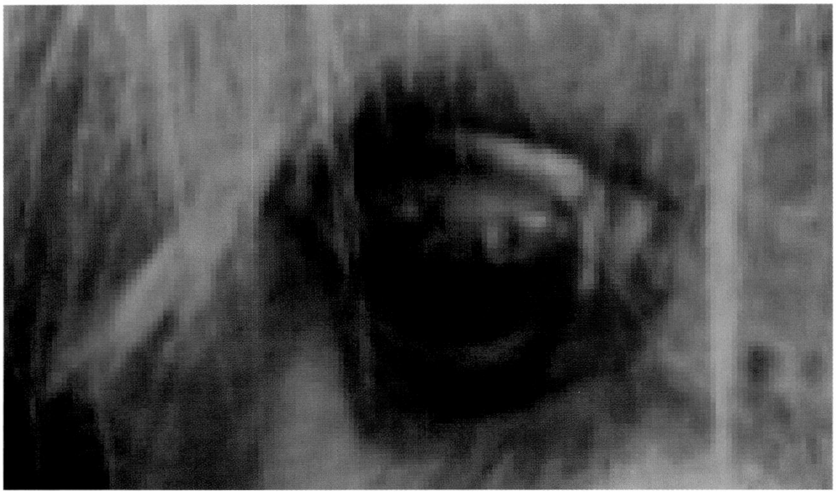

Unsharpened image
pixels at approximately
400 percent zoom

Figure 3-4
Source optimization for
a digital raw capture,
continued

*The entire image,
downsampled to print
size, optimized for
source*

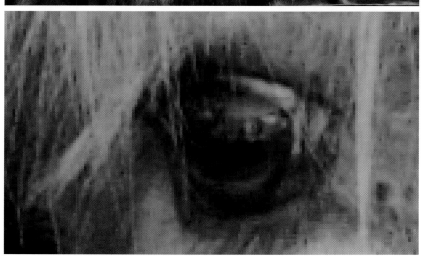

*Source-optimized image
detail at "contact print"
(300 ppi) resolution*

*Source-optimized image
pixels at approximately
400 percent zoom*

The difference between the unsharpened and sharpened versions is imperceptible on the image downsampled to print size, and barely perceptible on the "contact print" detail. On the 400 percent zoom view, however, the difference should be obvious. This is a very gentle sharpen indeed!

The salient features of this sharpening are:

▶ The sharpening radius is tuned to the minimum level of detail the camera can resolve.

▶ The sharpening is applied in luminosity blend mode to eliminate the possibility of color shifts.

▶ The sharpening is focused on the midtones, with nothing being sharpened below level 25 or above level 200.

Figure 3-5 shows the source optimization for a color negative. In this case, the focus is on noise reduction rather than sharpening. The goal in both cases is to improve the relationship between image detail and system noise, but the different capture media demand different treatments.

Figure 3-5   **Source optimization for color negative**

Before optimization, downsampled   *After optimization, downsampled*

Figure 3-5   Source optimization for color negative, *continued*

Before optimization, contact print   *After optimization, contact print*

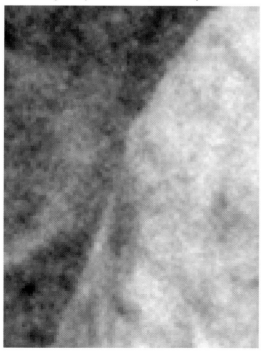

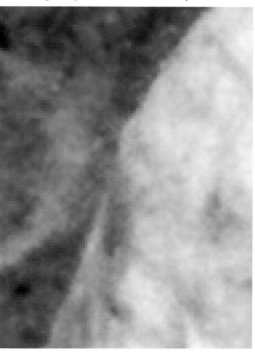

Before optimization, 400 percent zoom   *After optimization, 400 percent zoom*

I'll discuss specific techniques you can use to achieve these ends in Chapter 4, *Sharpening Tools and Techniques*. Photoshop invariably offers several different ways to accomplish any given task, and for the moment it's more important to understand the goals of the different stages in the workflow than it is to focus on the details of the techniques needed to attain those goals.

Reasonable people may question whether such barely perceptible edits as the ones shown in Figures 3-4 and 3-5 are actually useful. Bear in mind that the real goal of this step in the workflow is to improve the relationship between edges and noise so that the next step, sharpening for content through an edge mask, works optimally. So it's less about the image, and more about setting the image up to make a good sharpening mask!

Figure 3-6
Content optimization for
a high-frequency image

*The entire image,
downsampled to print
size, before content
sharpening*

*The entire image,
downsampled to print
size, after content
sharpening*

Optimizing for Image Content

As you saw in Chapter 2, *Why Do We Sharpen*, a busy, high-frequency image with lots of fine detail demands a different kind of sharpening than does a low-frequency image with soft, wide edges. This phase of the sharpening workflow is where that difference is taken into account.

Figure 3-6 shows the image from Figure 3-4 before and after content sharpening, along with the mask that was used to isolate the sharpening to the edges. The mask plays a dual role—it prevents sharpening areas of flat texture, leaving headroom for the final output sharpening, and it provides some control over the width of the sharpened edges.

Figure 3-6
Content optimization for
a high-frequency image,
continued

*Before content
sharpening at "contact
print" (300 ppi)
resolution*

*After content
sharpening at "contact
print" (300 ppi)
resolution*

Figure 3-6
Content optimization for
a high-frequency image,
continued

*The sharpening mask
through which the
content sharpening is
applied*

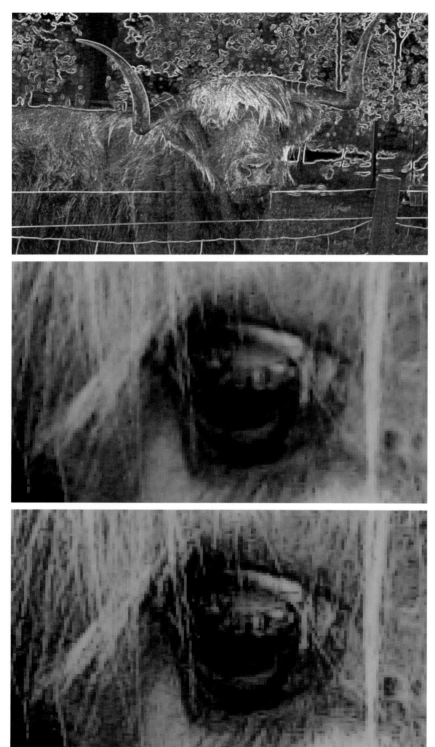

*Image pixels at
400 percent view before
content sharpening*

*Image pixels at
400 percent view after
content sharpening*

The layer mask offers some limited control over the width of the sharpening halo, but it's vital to match the actual sharpening settings to the image content rather than relying on the mask. I'll discuss techniques for building and applying layer masks, and applying sharpening through them, in Chapter 4, *Sharpening Tools and Techniques*. For now, it's enough to remember the simple rule that white reveals and black conceals. (Intermediate shades of gray, logically enough, apply varying opacities to the masked layer proportional to the shade of gray.)

The layer mask's real job is to protect the areas we don't want to sharpen at this stage, which is everything except the obvious edges. Note the qualifier, "obvious"—almost all images contain a mixture of low-frequency, mid-frequency, and high-frequency edges. You need to decide the dominant tendency and sharpen accordingly in this phase of the workflow.

Figure 3-7 shows the image from Figure 3-5 before and after sharpening for content through a layer mask. While the image contains mid-frequency and high-frequency details, the dominant tendency I chose to emphasize is the low-frequency edges, which are the most important in this image.

Figure 3-7   Content optimization for a low-frequency image

Before content optimization, downsampled   *After content optimization, downsampled*

Figure 3-7   Content optimization for a low-frequency image, *continued*

Before content optimization, contact print   *After content optimization, contact print*

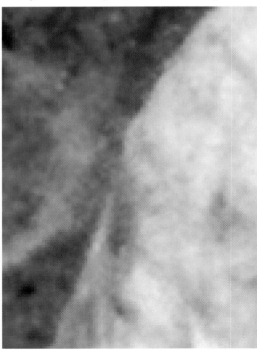 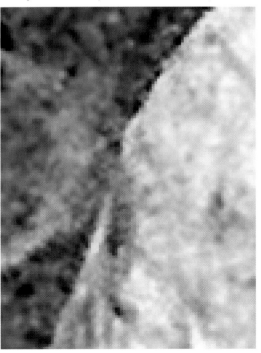

Before content optimization, 400 percent zoom   *After content optimization, 400 percent zoom*

Figure 3-7   Content optimization for a low-frequency image, *continued*

The layer mask

The effect of content sharpening is much more noticable, even on the downsampled image, than that of source optimization. Content optimization shares some of the properties of source optimization—the sharpening is applied in luminosity blend mode to eliminate the possibility of color shifts, and the sharpening is focused on the midtones, with nothing being sharpened below level 25 or above level 200—but in this step of the workflow, the sharpening radius is tuned to the image content we wish to emphasize rather than being dictated by the properties of the sensor.

Content sharpening sets the image up for output sharpening for specific uses, but it also provides two useful and important benefits.

Use-Neutral Master Images

The combination of source and content optimization produces a "use-neutral" master image that can be repurposed for different outputs. The optimized image can be downsampled or, to a lesser extent, upsampled, then sharpened for the specific use at hand. This is a very different model from the traditional sharpening workflow, where sharpening starts from scratch at every different use. The presharpened image becomes a digital asset, ready for a wide range of output uses.

Of course, there are limits. Film grain makes scanned images less amenable to resizing than digital captures, but experience suggests that I can upsample presharpened digital captures to 200 percent or downsample to 10 percent without additional handling beyond output sharpening.

Fixed Output Sharpening

A second benefit of this workflow is that, since all the image-specific and source-specific issues have already been addressed, output sharpening becomes a fixed, determinate process that requires no decision making. Since the relationship between input pixels and output dots (or output pixels if the output is to the display) is fixed—that is, it doesn't vary from image to image—it becomes possible to create optimal routines for output sharpening that do not and need not vary with image source or content.

In the future, such sharpening routines may be embedded in printer drivers or RIPs, where they can be applied automatically. (Many workflows already rely on in-RIP separations and in-RIP trapping, so in-RIP sharpening doesn't seem like much of a stretch.) At this stage in the workflow, the only factors that influence sharpening are

▶ The type of output (halftone, continuous-tone, inkjet, etc.)

▶ The image size and resolution

▶ The paper type—glossy/coated papers need slightly less sharpening than matte/uncoated ones to achieve the same apparent sharpness.

All these factors are known at print time, so output sharpening becomes a simple matter of selecting and running the appropriate routine. But before we get to output sharpening, there's another optional stage in the workflow, that of creative sharpening.

Creative Sharpening

Creative sharpening isn't required for every image (if you're shooting 500 plumbing widgets on white seamless backgrounds, creative sharpening probably isn't in the budget), but on some images, subtle sharpening (or blurring) moves can make a big difference.

For example, on head shots I often add a little extra sharpness to the eyes and hair. Sometimes skin texture needs a little softening. And of course, while one way to make a subject stand out from its surroundings is to sharpen it, it's sometimes more effective to blur the surroundings (which makes the subject appear sharper without actually sharpening it).

Figure 3-8 shows some examples of creative sharpening and blurring. They represent subjective decisions made on my part with which you may well disagree, but they serve to illustrate the point that localized control of detail can be a creative tool.

Figure 3-8
Creative sharpening

This is one of my favorite shots of my father, but the bench sticking out of his head is intrusive to say the least!

Before creative sharpening

I improved the image by darkening the bench, applying some extra sharpening to the face and hair, and blurring the background slightly.

After creative sharpening

Figure 3-8
Creative sharpening,
continued

The final image after output sharpening. The creative sharpening and blurring adjustments improve the separation between subject and background.

After final output sharpening

In this (much better) photograph of my father's son (can you see the resemblance?), the skin texture is a little too much—it distracts the eye.

I added some sharpness to both eyes (more to the distant one than to the close one), and softened the skin texture slightly. Both images were then sharpened for final output.

There are few rules for creative sharpening beyond those dictated by taste: You have to learn the behavior of your display so that you can make reasonable judgments as to how far to push the sharpening, and there's no shortcut for doing that.

As with all the previous steps in the sharpening workflow, it's a good idea to leave headroom for the final output sharpening by protecting the extreme highlights and shadows, and to do your creative sharpening on the native-resolution image. I'll discuss specific techniques for creative sharpening in Chapter 4, *Sharpening Tools and Techniques*.

Output Sharpening

The final step in the sharpening workflow compensates both for softening introduced by the output process, and for softening induced by resizing to final output resolution. At this stage in the workflow, all the other factors that affect sharpening have already been addressed, so this step can focus (no pun intended) entirely on the output process.

Since the relationship between input pixels and output dots is always the same, it's possible to create a single optimal sharpening routine for each output process and resolution. It's true that different platesetters or different inkjet printers use subtly different screening algorithms, but all we can do is to sharpen the pixels—we can't control how they get turned into dots—and in practice, these small differences are below the threshold that we can address by sharpening pixels.

Matte papers may need slightly more sharpening than glossy or luster papers to achieve the same apparent sharpness, since the ink bleeds a little more on matte papers, but the difference is quite small, and it's up to you to decide whether it's worthwhile making separate sharpening routines for the same device on matte and glossy papers. It's almost certainly overkill to make more than two paper-specific routines.

By far the most important factor is the pixel resolution you send to print, because it dictates the size of the pixels, and hence the size of the sharpening haloes. Up to this point in the workflow, we've tried to avoid obvious sharpening haloes. For output sharpening, however, we want haloes that may be obvious on the computer display when viewed at actual pixels (or higher) zoom, but that will still fall below the threshold of visual acuity at reasonable viewing distance for the print.

Unlike all the previous sharpening passes, output sharpening is applied globally to the entire image, with no masking, and to the entire tonal range without protecting the highlights and shadows. It's by far the simplest of the sharpening passes, but it's a vital one.

Output Sharpening in Practice

In this book, I'm limited to showing the output sharpening for the 150-line screen used to print it. But within these constraints, I *can* show how output sharpening interacts with the previous stages of the sharpening workflow on the same images downsampled to different resolutions.

Figure 3-9 shows several versions of an image. All versions were produced from the same native-resolution master file. The only differences are in the output resolution and the output sharpening that accommodates it, and whether or not it had been optimized for source and content.

Output sharpening is very much like traditional prepress sharpening. You'll see that the versions without optimization for source and content aren't unacceptably soft, but you'll also see that the optimized versions are sharper, without appearing oversharpened. The optimizations for source and content allow me to take the same master file and produce optimally sharp versions of the image at different sizes and resolutions simply by downsampling and applying the appropriate output sharpeners.

Output Sharpening and the Display

Just to round out the picture, Figure 3-9 also shows a zoomed detail of the optimized-and-output-sharpened image that corresponds roughly to viewing the image pixels on screen at 400 percent zoom. I included these views not because attempting to judge sharpness by looking at pixels at 400 percent zoom is a useful or even rational activity—it isn't—but simply to dramatize the fact that images that are well sharpened for output will almost certainly look scary on the computer display.

As I explained back in Chapter 2, *Why Do We Sharpen?*, it's just about impossible to judge final print sharpness from the display. At the risk of some redundancy, I reiterate the point here because it bears repeating. One of the biggest leaps of faith in the entire Photoshop universe is sending pixels that looks hideous on screen to a printing device, but if the pixels don't look seriously crunchy on the display, you're almost certainly undersharpening your images. The only reliable way to evaluate print sharpening is to sharpen the image, print it, and look at the print!

Figure 3-9
Output sharpening

The image with no optimization for source or content, after downsampling to print size at 300 ppi and sharpening for 150-line screen output

The same image with optimization for source and content, after downsampling to print size at 300 ppi and sharpening for 150-line screen output

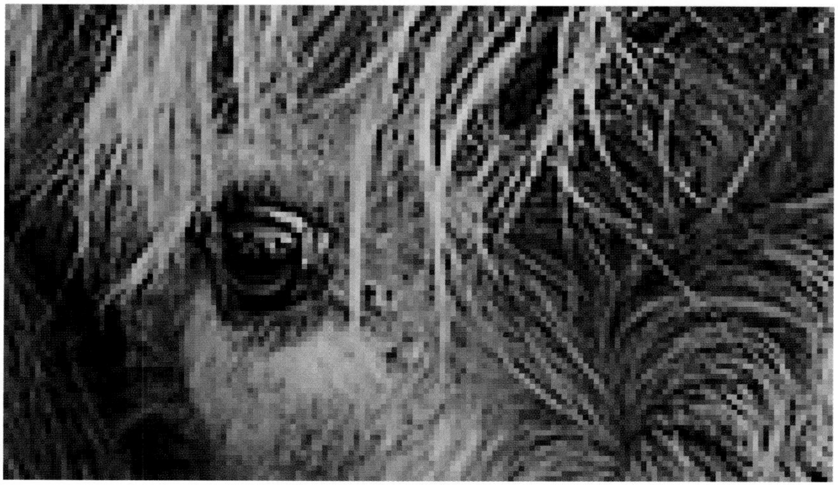

The optimized, output-sharpened image pixels at approximately 400 percent zoom

Figure 3-9
Output sharpening,
continued

*The image with no
optimization for source
or content, after
downsampling to
print size at 225 ppi
and sharpening for
150-line screen output*

*The same image with
optimization for source
and content, after
downsampling to
print size at 225 ppi
and sharpening for
150-line screen output*

*The optimized, output-
sharpened image pixels
at approximately 400
percent zoom*

Figure 3-9
Output sharpening,
continued

*Image detail at native
resolution, with no
optimization for source
or content, sharpened
for 150-line screen
output*

*The same image detail
with optimization for
source and content, after
sharpening for
150-line screen output*

*The optimized, output-
sharpened image pixels
at approximately 400
percent zoom*

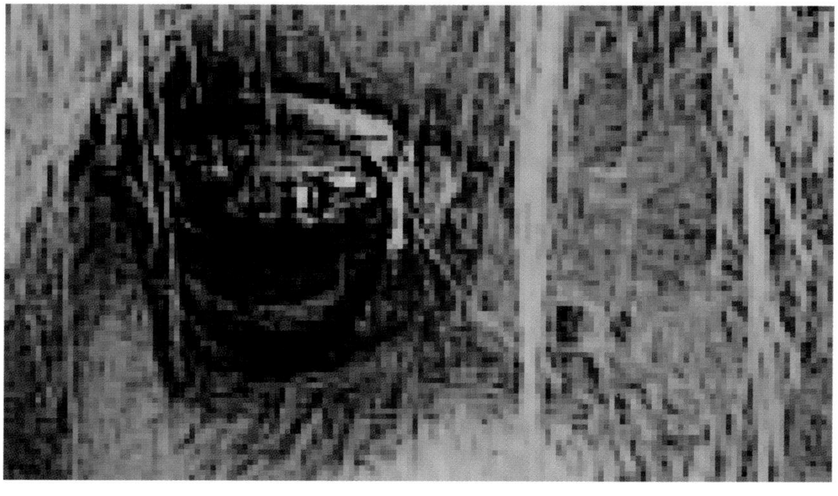

From Theory to Practice

Thus far, the focus of this book has been to expound the theory of a workflow-based approach to sharpening images. In the ensuing chapters, I'll shift that focus to concentrate on the practical application of the theory. Good sharpening requires mastery of a significant body of technique, and knowledge of some of the murkier depths of Photoshop, so in Chapter 4, *Sharpening Tools and Techniques*, I'll cover all the techniques and tricks that I use in my own sharpening workflow, including nondestructive layer-based sharpening, and the all-important use of layer masks.

4

Sharpening Tools and Techniques

Learning to Sharpen

Thus far, this book has been fairly long on theory and short on practice. In this chapter, I'll switch focus to looking in depth at the tools Photoshop offers for sharpening images, and the techniques you need to develop in order to use them effectively in a capture-to-output sharpening workflow. The tools themselves are important, but there's a world of difference between simply running the Unsharp Mask filter on a flattened image and running Unsharp Mask on a layer with an edge mask: the former uses a tool, while the latter employs a technique.

So in this chapter, I'll explain the basic tools, but I'll also demonstrate techniques for using those tools in ways that may not be obvious. Of course, Photoshop always offers multiple ways to carry out any given task. It's not my intention to cover every possible way to sharpen pixels. To do so would greatly lengthen this book, and take us into territories that my friend and colleague Fred Bunting eloquently describes as "more interesting than relevant."

Instead, I'll cover the tools and techniques that I've tested exhaustively, that I use on a daily basis, and in which I have total confidence. If a cherished trick of yours isn't covered here, don't worry—it's entirely possible that you know something I don't. By the same token, if I debunk a cherished myth, rest assured that I do so without malice—at some point in time, they were very likely myths that I, too, cherished.

Sharpening Tools

Photoshop offers a variety of sharpening tools, ranging from the indispensable Unsharp Mask to the extremely hard to control Sharpen tool. But Photoshop also offers ways to sharpen images using features that don't provide any hint by their names that sharpening is one of their capabilities. Everyone has their preferred sets of tools, but few of us actually spend time analyzing what they do, so before examining the tools themselves, let me show you an easy way to see the effects of different sharpening routines.

Analyzing Sharpeners

One very easy way to compare the effect of different sharpening routines is to look at what they do to a variety of edges with different contrast. Figure 4-1 shows a simple test file that you can make yourself, which contains a single edge with varying contrast from solid black on white to midtone gray on midtone gray.

Figure 4-1
Sharpener analysis target

There are (of course) several ways to create a target like this. For on-screen use (which is what this target is best for), I do the following:

► Create a new document, either RGB or Grayscale, 512 pixels wide by 50 pixels tall.

► Fill it with a black-to-white gradient using the Gradient tool.

► Select either the top or the bottom half of the image (the selection should be 512 pixels by 25 pixels—you can use the Info palette and/or the rulers to get the selection the right size).

► Invert the selected area (Image>Adjustments>Invert, or press Command-I).

► Finally, crop the image in half horizontally from the right edge to obtain an image that looks like Figure 4-1, 256 pixels wide by 50 pixels tall.

If you zoom to around 400% or 500% the target will still fit most screens and you can easily see what happens at the pixel level. This target helps you understand what different sharpening tools do to edges, with the important caveat that their behavior on real images may be more complex than on this simple target.

Sharpen

Located on the Filter>Sharpen submenu, the Sharpen filter applies a simple, nonadjustable sharpening routine that creates a single-pixel halo for the light contour and a single-pixel halo for the dark contour. The haloes reach maximum intensity (solid black and pure white) when the difference between the light and dark sides of the edge is 169 levels.

Sharpen is virtually identical to running the Unsharp Mask filter (discussed later in this chapter) with Amount 130, Radius 0.4, and Threshold 0. Figure 4-2 shows the target from Figure 4-1 after applying the Sharpen filter.

Figure 4-2
The Sharpen filter

Sharpen More

As its name suggests, Sharpen More is a stronger version of Sharpen. It also creates a single-pixel halo, but reaches maximum intensity sooner, when the difference betwen the light and dark sides of the edges is 85 levels.

Sharpen More is virtually identical to running the Unsharp Mask filter with Amount at 390, Radius at 0.4, and Threshold at 0. Figure 4-3 shows the target from Figure 4-1 after applying the Sharpen More filter.

Figure 4-3
The Sharpen More filter

I personally never use these filters since I can obtain the same results using the Unsharp Mask filter.

Sharpen Edges

Sharpen Edges, which appears on the Sharpen submenu of the Filter menu in between Sharpen and Sharpen More, is a little different inasmuch as its effect can't be replicated exactly using Unsharp Mask. However, Unsharp Mask with Amount at 140, Radius at 0.4, and Threshold at 3 comes very close—the Unsharp Mask produces very slightly stronger contrast in the midtones. Like Sharpen, Sharpen Edges reaches maximum intensity at a difference of 169 levels. The main difference between the two is that Sharpen Edges has a gentler start on values that differ only slightly.

Sharpen Edges isn't really any more useful than Sharpen or Sharpen More—the difference between what it does and what I can accomplish with Unsharp Mask is so small as to be merely academically interesting, and the lack of control makes it inflexible. Figure 4-4 shows the target from Figure 4-1 after applying the Sharpen Edges filter.

Figure 4-4
The Sharpen Edges filter

If the first three entries on the Filter>Sharpen submenu are mostly of academic interest, the last two, Smart Sharpen and Unsharp Mask, are essential sharpening tools. However, it's just about impossible to understand Smart Sharpen until you've mastered Unsharp Mask, so I'll discuss Unsharp Mask first.

Unsharp Mask

The Unsharp Mask filter is by far the most important item in the sharpening toolbox—if I were forced to rely on a single sharpening tool, I'd choose Unsharp Mask for its speed, power, and flexibility. In short, Unsharp Mask is indispensable!

Unlike Sharpen, Sharpen Edges, and Sharpen More, all of which simply apply preset routines, the Unsharp Mask filter offers a great deal of control over sharpening. Figure 4-5 shows the Unsharp Mask filter dialog box at its default settings, Amount at 100, Radius at 1, Threshold at 0. Mastery of these three controls, Amount, Radius, and Threshold, is key to good sharpening.

Figure 4-5
The Unsharp Mask
dialog box

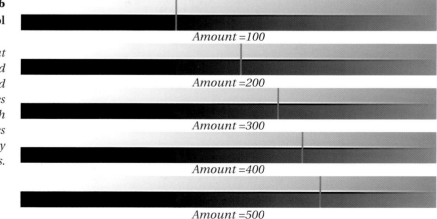

▶ **Amount** controls the intensity of the sharpening haloes—the increase in contrast along edges.

▶ **Radius** controls the width of the sharpening haloes.

▶ **Threshold** controls the onset of the sharpening haloes—the degree of contrast between pixels that makes Unsharp Mask treat them as representing an edge.

Together, these controls offer a huge amount of control over sharpening.

Amount sets the intensity of the sharpening halo. At low settings, it takes more difference between levels for the sharpening haloes to reach pure white and solid black; at higher settings, it takes less difference. Figure 4-6 shows the effect of the Amount slider at constant Radius and Threshold settings.

Figure 4-6
The Amount control

The Amount slider at 100, 200, 300, 400, and 500, with Radius 0.4 and Threshold 0. The red lines indicate the point at which the sharpening haloes reach maximum intensity at the selected Radius.

Amount =100

Amount =200

Amount =300

Amount =400

Amount =500

Radius is the control that sets the width of the sharpening haloes, though it also has some effect on their intensity. However, since it was designed by engineers rather than photographers, the number you enter into the Radius field doesn't actually produce haloes of that size (not that it's possible to produce a sharpening halo 0.4 pixels wide).

What the Radius setting actually does is a little more complicated. The Unsharp Mask filter changes pixels one at a time, examining the surrounding pixels to determine the difference in contrast between the subject pixel and its neighbors. The Radius setting tells the filter how many surrounding pixels to take into account when calculating the new value for the subject pixel.

The net effect, however, is that low Radius settings produce narrow sharpening haloes and higher settings produce wider ones. (At very high settings, the sharpening haloes collide and merge into one another, so the effect changes from a pure sharpening to an overall contrast adjustment—see "Midtone Contrast," later in this chapter.)

Figure 4-7 shows the effect of the Radius setting at constant Amount and Threshold settings. (I've zoomed and cropped the target to exclude the higher-contrast edges so that the difference between settings is more obvious.) Lower settings produce narrower haloes, higher settings produce wider ones, but the width of the haloes also depends on the contrast of the edge that's being sharpened.

Notice also that the intensity of the haloes increases with Radius—at higher settings, the sharpening haloes reach solid black and pure white earlier than they do at lower settings. However, Radius has a much smaller effect on intensity than does Amount.

The Radius control determines the "flavor" of the sharpening. Low-frequency images with wide edges and soft detail require higher Radius settings than high-frequency images with narrow edges and sharp tonal transitions. When I sharpen images for content, matching the Radius setting to the edges in the image is one of the most important aspects of the sharpening.

One aspect of Unsharp Mask that's less than optimal is the fact that it increases the width of the sharpening haloes as the contrast of the edge being sharpened increases. This is rarely the behavior I want. I'll discuss techniques for exercising additional control over the results produced by Unsharp Mask later in this chapter.

Figure 4-7
The Radius control

With Amount at 200 and
Threshold at 0, the
figures at right show the
effect of the Radius
setting at (from top
to bottom) 0.4, 0.8, 1,
1.2, 1.5, 2, 3, and 5,
respectively.

The red line shows the
point at which the
sharpening haloes reach
maximum intensity.

The width of the haloes
increases with contrast
at any single Radius
setting.

Threshold delays the onset of the sharpening haloes by telling the Unsharp Mask filter to ignore a certain amount of difference between pixels before applying any sharpening. Figure 4-8 shows the effect of the Threshold setting at constant settings for Radius and Amount—I've cropped the target to show the areas of interest.

Figure 4-8
The Threshold control

With Amount at 200 and Radius at 0.4, the figures at right show the effect of the Threshold setting.

The red line shows the point at which the sharpening haloes reach maximum intensity.

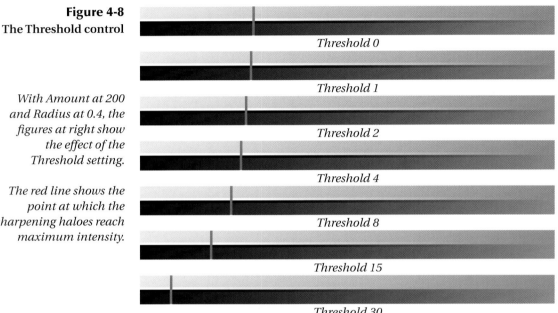

Threshold 0

Threshold 1

Threshold 2

Threshold 4

Threshold 8

Threshold 15

Threshold 30

The Threshold control is designed to allow you to protect textured areas such as skin tones or slightly noisy skies from being sharpened. At low settings (1–4), it works reasonably well on lightly textured areas, but may not provide enough protection. At higher settings, it has a tendency to create unnatural-looking transitions between the sharpened and unsharpened areas. Because of this tendency, I tend to rely on layer masks to protect textured areas rather than using Threshold. I'll cover techniques for doing so later in this chapter.

Working the controls. Whether I apply Unsharp Mask globally or through a layer mask, I always set the Radius first, because more than either of the controls, it dictates the character of the sharpening. Many different combinations of Amount and Radius produce the same apparent amount of sharpening, but with subtly different characteristics.

As you increase the Radius, you need to reduce the Amount, and vice versa, to maintain the same degree of apparent sharpness. Figure 4-9 shows the same image detail with two very different Unsharp Mask settings that nevertheless produce approximately the same degree of sharpness.

Figure 4-9
Amount and Radius

Unsharp Mask with Amount 130, Radius 1.1, Threshold 0

Unsharp Mask with Amount 500, Radius 0.4, Threshold 0

The difference between the two versions above is extremely subtle—I'd be surprised if you can see it—but that subtle difference becomes more obvious when a second round of sharpening is applied for the output. Figure 4-10 shows the same image detail sharpened for output, along with a zoomed-in view of the output-sharpened pixels.

Before output sharpening, the two versions seemed identical, but after output sharpening we begin to see subtle differences. The high-frequency detail on the birch bark at the upper left is revealed more clearly in the lower, small-radius version, than in the upper, larger-radius version, as is the puff-ball. Examination of the zoomed-in pixels confirms this—the detail on the puff-ball has higher contrast, and hence is more visible, in the upper, small-radius version than in the lower, larger-radius one.

Figure 4-10 shows something else important: while targets like the one first shown in Figure 4-1 can help us understand a good deal about the basic behavior of sharpening tools, the application of those tools to real

Figure 4-10
Amount and Radius with
output sharpening

Unsharp Mask with
Amount 130, Radius 1.1,
Threshold 0

Unsharp Mask with
Amount 500, Radius 0.4,
Threshold 0

photographic images is a good deal more complicated than to the target, because edges in real images are often more complex than a single row of dark pixels against a single row of white pixels.

So, while the behavior of the target might lead you to expect that the versions of the image in Figure 4-10 that were sharpened with a Radius setting of 1.1 might feature wider sharpening haloes than the one sharpened with a Radius setting of 0.4, in practice what happens is that the haloes have essentially the same width in both versions, because the image edges themselves constrain the width of the haloes. The higher-Radius version simply ends up with weaker contrast on the haloes.

Figure 4-10
Amount and Radius with
output sharpening,
continued

Unsharp Mask with Amount 130, Radius 1.1, Threshold 0

Unsharp Mask with Amount 500, Radius 0.4, Threshold 0

Unsharp Mask Limitations. Unsharp Mask is an immensely useful and powerful tool, but it suffers from two significant limitations:

▶ The Threshold control isn't terribly good at protecting noisy or lightly textured areas from sharpening. At low settings, it may not provide enough protection, while at higher settings it can produce unnatural-looking transitions. More significantly, the Threshold control wipes out midtone sharpening, which is often where we need it most.

▶ Unsharp Mask always sharpens high-contrast edges more than low-contrast ones, which is usually the exact opposite of the behavior we need. On edges that are already at maximum (solid black and pure white) contrast, Unsharp Mask simply widens the sharpening halo, a behavior that's almost always undesirable.

I'll discuss techniques for dealing with these problems later in this chapter, but first, let's look at Smart Sharpen, which also tries, in its own way, to address these issues.

Smart Sharpen

The Smart Sharpen filter is a good deal more complex than the Unsharp Mask filter since it offers more options. Figure 4-11 shows the Smart Sharpen dialog box in Basic mode.

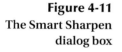
Figure 4-11
The Smart Sharpen
dialog box

Smart Sharpen has no Threshold control, only Radius and Amount, but the additional controls it offers add up to many different permutations.

▶ The Basic and Advanced radio buttons control whether or not the Shadow and Highlight tabs become available. In Advanced mode, these two additional tabs let you shape the tonality of the light and dark contours, allowing you to reduce the sharpening on high-contrast edges—see Figure 4-12.

▶ The Remove menu lets you choose one of three flavors of sharpening. Remove Gaussian Blur works essentially the same as Unsharp Mask; Remove Lens Blur uses a different sharpening algorithm that attempts to differentiate actual edges from image noise; Remove Motion Blur lets you (within limits) undo motion blur caused by subject or camera movement.

▶ Checking the More Accurate checkbox makes the filter run more iterations, producing a significantly different result than when it's unchecked. It also makes the filter run a little more slowly.

Figure 4-12
The Smart Sharpen
Advanced dialog box,
Shadow and Highlight
tabs

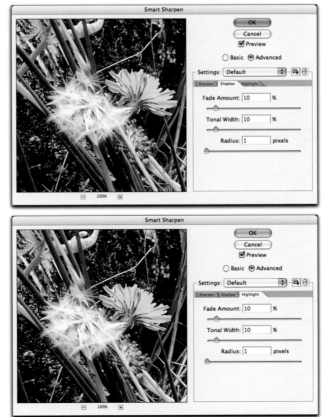

Gaussian Blur. When Gaussian Blur is selected from the Remove menu, the More Accurate checkbox is unchecked, and the filter is in Basic mode, it behaves identically to Unsharp Mask with the same Amount and Radius settings and Threshold at 0.

When the More Accurate checkbox is checked, the filter behavior changes, producing a wider halo with gentler contrast. Figure 4-13 shows the difference between Gaussian Blur, Basic mode, with More Accurate unchecked (which is the same as Unsharp Mask), and Gaussian Blur, Basic mode, with More Accurate checked.

Figure 4-13
Smart Sharpen, Remove
Gaussian Blur, Basic
mode, with and without
More Accurate

When More Accurate is unchecked (upper image), Smart Sharpen with Gaussian Blur behaves exactly like Unsharp Mask. When More Accurate is checked (lower image), Smart Sharpen produces a wider, lower-contrast halo. The red line indicates where the sharpening haloes reach maximum intensity.

On real images, Gaussian Blur with More Accurate checked produces much weaker sharpening than when it's unchecked, so much so that small-radius sharpening is very weak indeed. Figure 4-14 shows an image detail that had Smart Sharpening applied for content before being sharpened for output, using Amount 500 and Radius 0.4, with More Accurate unchecked, and with More Accurate checked.

Both versions are acceptable, but the one that had More Accurate unchecked ("Less Accurate?") has a little more snap. Numerous similar examples have led me to conclude that in the majority of cases, Smart Sharpen with Gaussian Blur in Basic mode offers little or no advantage over Unsharp Mask.

Gaussian Blur Advanced Mode. When the Advanced radio button is selected, the Shadow and Highlight tabs (see Figure 4-12) become active. These tabs let you fade the contrast of the dark and light sharpening contours, respectively.

Figure 4-14
Smart Sharpen, Remove Gaussian Blur, Basic mode, with and without More Accurate

Smart Sharpen, Amount 500, Radius 0.4, More Accurate unchecked, followed by output sharpening

Smart Sharpen, Amount 500, Radius 0.4, More Accurate checked, followed by output sharpening

Both tabs offer the same three controls; Fade Amount, Tonal Width, and Radius, which together determine the way the Shadow (dark) and Highlight (light) contours along edges have their intensity reduced.

▶ **Fade Amount** controls the degree of fading of the Shadow or Highlight contour.

▶ **Tonal Width** controls the tonal range across which the fade applies, starting from solid black (level 0) for the Shadow contour and pure white (level 255) for the Highlight contour.

▶ **Radius** works akin to the Radius control in Photoshop's Shadow/Highlight image adjustment command, specifying the neighborhood the filter evaluates in determining whether or not a pixel is a Shadow or Highlight pixel and hence is affected by the settings in the Shadow and Highlight tabs.

When used in conjunction with Gaussian Blur, the effect of the Radius setting is barely detectable (and is only detectable by doing actual pixel-value comparisons—you can't see it). However, it has an obvious effect, not on the image, but on the speed of the filter—it's much, much slower at high Radius settings than at lower ones!

Figure 4-15 shows the effect of the Advanced mode options at several different settings. The difference between (Advanced) Radius set at 1 and the much slower (Advanced) Radius set at 100 is detectable, though not terribly visually significant, when the Tonal Width is set to a low amount, but it's basically insignificant at higher Tonal Width settings.

The ability to fade the highlight and shadow contours, and thus force more of the sharpening into the midtones, is useful for early-stage sharpening

Figure 4-15
Smart Sharpen, Gaussian Blur, Basic and Advanced modes

These figures differ only in the Advanced options. All were made with Amount at 500 and Radius at 0.4. The Fade Amount, Tonal Width, and Advanced Radius settings were applied equally in the Shadow and Highlight tabs.

The red lines indicate the maximum intensity of the sharpening haloes—in some cases, it's a range.

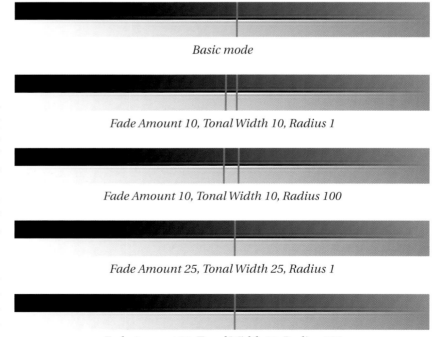

Basic mode

Fade Amount 10, Tonal Width 10, Radius 1

Fade Amount 10, Tonal Width 10, Radius 100

Fade Amount 25, Tonal Width 25, Radius 1

Fade Amount 25, Tonal Width 25, Radius 100

for image content, but you can lose a lot of time fiddling with settings that make almost no difference to the result! See "Sharpening Tonal Ranges," later in this chapter, for a technique that provides most of the benefits of Smart Sharpen's Advanced mode using plain old Unsharp Mask.

Lens Blur. Choosing Lens Blur from the Remove menu makes Smart Sharpen use a different algorithm that sharpens the midtones rather more aggressively than either Unsharp Mask or Smart Sharpen with Gaussian Blur. The More Accurate and Advanced options modulate the effect of the sharpening much like they do when Gaussian Blur is selected.

Figure 4-16 compares the the Lens Blur and Gaussian Blur "flavors" of sharpening at two different strengths, with More Accurate on and off.

Figure 4-16
Smart Sharpen,
Gaussian Blur, and
Lens Blur compared

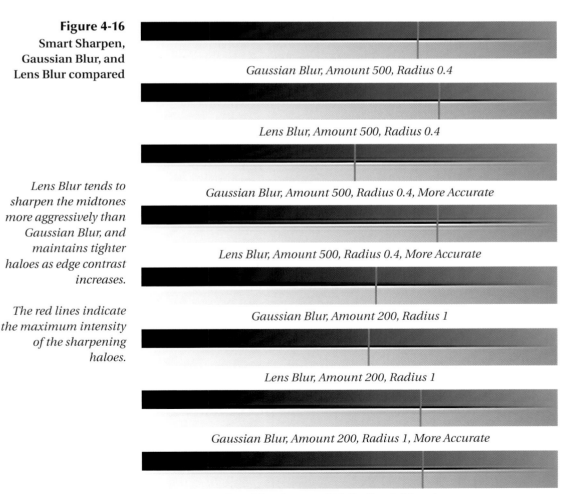

Gaussian Blur, Amount 500, Radius 0.4

Lens Blur, Amount 500, Radius 0.4

Gaussian Blur, Amount 500, Radius 0.4, More Accurate

Lens Blur, Amount 500, Radius 0.4, More Accurate

Gaussian Blur, Amount 200, Radius 1

Lens Blur, Amount 200, Radius 1

Gaussian Blur, Amount 200, Radius 1, More Accurate

Lens Blur, Amount 200, Radius 1, More Accurate

Lens Blur tends to sharpen the midtones more aggressively than Gaussian Blur, and maintains tighter haloes as edge contrast increases.

The red lines indicate the maximum intensity of the sharpening haloes.

The More Accurate option works approximately the same with Lens Blur as it does with Gaussian Blur, making a slightly wider but gentler sharpening halo. But the most obvious difference between Gaussian Blur and Lens Blur is that the latter does a much better job of controlling the width of the halo along high-contrast edges than does Gaussian Blur, which creates ever-widening haloes as contrast increases.

Lens Blur Advanced Mode. The Advanced option enables Smart Sharpen's Shadow and Highlight tabs, allowing you to fade the light and dark contours of the sharpening haloes. The controls operate similarly to the way they do with Gaussian Blur (including the dramatic slowdown produced by high Radius settings in the Shadow and Highlight tabs), but the effect of the Shadow and Highlight Radius settings is a little more discernible than with Gaussian Blur, as shown in Figure 4-17.

With Lens Blur, the Advanced options do a better job of sharpening midtones while protecting extreme highlights and shadows than they do with Gaussian Blur. But the effects of the Radius setting are still quite subtle, and the extreme slowdowns caused by high Radius settings in the Shadow and Highlight tabs provide an exercise in frustration. Figure 4-18 shows the same image detail sharpened with Smart Sharpen using Radius 1 and Radius 100 in the Advanced tabs, then sharpened for output, along with a version that used Unsharp Mask for the preliminary sharpening.

Figure 4-17
Smart Sharpen, Lens Blur, Basic and Advanced modes
These figures differ only in the Advanced options. All were made with Amount at 500 and Radius at 0.4. The Advanced options were applied equally in the Shadow and Highlight tabs.

The red lines indicate the maximum intensity of the sharpening haloes—in some cases, it's a range.

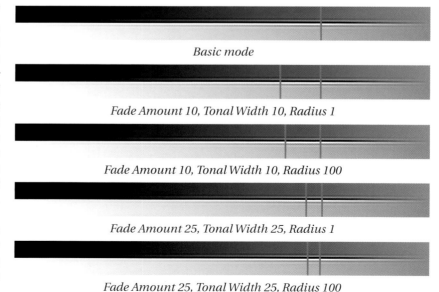

Basic mode

Fade Amount 10, Tonal Width 10, Radius 1

Fade Amount 10, Tonal Width 10, Radius 100

Fade Amount 25, Tonal Width 25, Radius 1

Fade Amount 25, Tonal Width 25, Radius 100

Figure 4-18
Smart Sharpen and
Unsharp Mask

*Smart Sharpen with
Lens Blur, Amount
500, Radius 0.4, Fade
Amount 25, Tonal Width
25, Radius 1*

*Smart Sharpen with
Lens Blur, Amount
500, Radius 0.4, Fade
Amount 25, Tonal Width
25, Radius 100*

*Unsharp Mask,
Amount 500, Radius 0.3*

Smart Sharpen does a good job on the high-frequency detail (though the difference between Radius 1 and Radius 100 in the Advanced tabs is very subtle indeed), but copes less well with the soft edges of the puff-ball. I cheated slightly on the Unsharp Mask version, duplicating the Background layer, sharpening it with Unsharp Mask, then using the Blend If sliders in the Layer Options dialog box to fade the extreme shadow and highlight contours—I'll explore this technique in detail in "Sharpening Tonal Ranges," later in this chapter.

Warning: Advanced Options Persist Even When Hidden. One of the more infuriating aspects of Smart Sharpen is that switching from Advanced to Basic mode doesn't actually turn off the settings in the Shadow and Highlight tabs—it just hides them. So it's all too easy to fade the highlights and shadows without meaning to. The only safe solution is to *always* use Advanced mode, and *always* check the settings in the Shadow and Highlight tabs before doing anything else. Otherwise you may find yourself getting entirely unexpected results.

Motion Blur. The third and final Smart Sharpen flavor, Motion Blur, is (as its name suggests) designed to undo motion blur caused by subject or camera movement. Don't expect miracles—those only happen on TV crime shows—but with care, Smart Sharpen with Motion Blur can do a reasonable job of extracting detail from a moving subject. Figure 4-19 shows one such example.

When Motion Blur is selected from the Remove menu, one additional control, Angle, becomes enabled. The Angle setting is the key parameter in using Smart Sharpen's Motion Blur mode to undo motion blur. Once the Angle is correct, the next step is to set the Radius and Amount, followed by the options in the Shadow and Highlight tabs.

Unlike the other Smart Sharpen flavors, Motion Blur rarely works when it's applied to an entire image. It's best used for un-blurring specific subjects in the image, and the work goes much faster if you make a rough selection of the subject, then copy it to a new layer. Once the sharpening is applied, you can either erase the unwanted areas from the rough selection, or mask them using a layer mask as I did in the example shown in Figure 4-19.

Figure 4-19
Smart Sharpen with
Motion Blur

The original image

*The image after Smart
Sharpen with Motion
Blur, using the settings
shown below*

Smart Sharpen issues. Smart Sharpen is an intriguing tool that has won its share of devotees. I confess that I can't number myself among them. I do use Smart Sharpen for some tasks—the Motion Blur option is the only game in town for undoing motion blur, and Smart Sharpen works very well indeed for on-screen output, which typically involves fairly small files. On print-resolution images, however, Smart Sharpen is often infuriatingly slow.

The persistence of the Shadow and Highlight settings when the filter has been switched back to Basic mode has undoubtedly caused a great deal of head-scratching, and is at best a questionable design decision. And while the Shadow and Highlight tabs attempt to address a real issue—reducing the intensity of the highlight and shadow contours—they simply don't offer the degree of control I need. As a result, I still rely on the Unsharp Mask filter for the majority of my sharpening tasks.

However, it's relatively rare for me to simply apply Unsharp Mask globally to an image. Instead, I use the techniques described in the next section. At first glance, they may seem to require more work than Smart Sharpen, but much of that work can be automated, and the actual routines run quite quickly.

Sharpening Techniques

Knowing your way around Photoshop's sharpening tools is a good start, but learning how to deploy them is the key to mastering sharpening, especially if you plan to use the workflow-based approach to sharpening that I outlined in the previous chapter. Multipass sharpening has to be approached with care and diligence, otherwise it's all too easy to end up with an oversharpened mess.

So in this section, I'll describe techniques for controlling sharpening not only while it's being applied, but also after it's been applied. I'll show you how to sharpen nondestructively, so that if things go horribly wrong you still have an escape route. I'll show you how to confine your sharpening to specific tonal ranges, and image areas, so that you can sharpen edges without affecting textured areas or sharpening noise, and how to make sharpening brushes for different types of creative sharpening. Last but not least, I'll look at techniques for reducing noise so that it doesn't interfere wth the sharpening process.

The Sharpen Tool

The Sharpen tool shares a slot in Photoshop's toolbox with the Blur tool and the Sponge tool. At its default setting of 50% opacity, it applies sharpening that is similar (but not identical) to the Sharpen filter—it's a little more aggressive in the midtones than Sharpen.

Used sparingly, at low opacities, the Sharpen tool is moderately useful for adding a slight increase in sharpness to a specific area in the image. But caution is most definitely required, because repeated applications of the Sharpen tool can quickly destroy images!

Figure 4-20 shows the results of the Sharpen tool applied up to five times. A single-pixel halo quickly turns into a grid of parallel lines. I'll show you how to make more controllable sharpening brushes in "Sharpening Brushes," later in this chapter.

Figure 4-20
The Sharpen tool

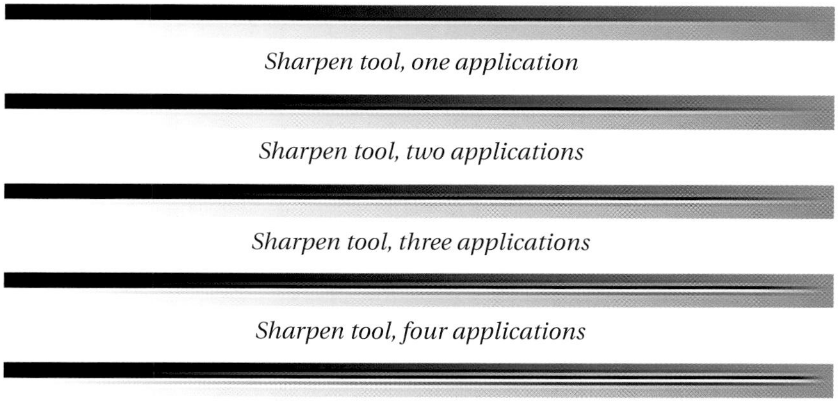

Sharpen tool, one application

Sharpen tool, two applications

Sharpen tool, three applications

Sharpen tool, four applications

Sharpen tool, five applications

Sharpening on a Layer

When you run Unsharp Mask on a flat image, you have very limited control after you've applied the sharpening. You can immediately use the Fade command to reduce the strength of the sharpening or to apply it with a blend mode, but a single mouse-click renders Fade unavailable.

If, instead, you sharpen on a layer, a whole range of post-sharpening tweaks become available, and much of this section is devoted to these tweaks. But before you can run, you must learn to walk, so first let's look at the basics of creating sharpening layers. There are really only two ways.

▶ If the image is a flat file, simply duplicate the Background layer.

▶ If the image is a layered file, press Option while choosing Merge Visible from the Layer menu or press Command-Option-Shift-E. (See Figure 4-21 for both methods.)

Figure 4-21
Creating a
sharpening layer

On a flat file...   *Drag the*   *...to the New Layer*   *...to create a*
                       Background layer...   *icon in the Layers*   *sharpening layer*
                                            palette...

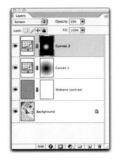

On a layered file...

Hold down Option
(Mac) or Alt (Windows)
while choosing Merge
Visible from the Layer
menu...

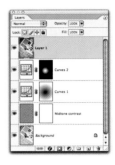

...to create a
sharpening layer

You can then apply sharpening to the new layer, leaving the Background or underlying layers untouched.

Performing sharpening on a layer opens up several possibilities that aren't available when you simply burn sharpening into the pixels on a flat file. For example, you can tweak the strength of the sharpening by adjusting the opacity of the sharpening layer using the Layer Opacity slider in the Layers palette. This is particularly useful when you're trying to blend localized creative sharpening into an image that has already had base sharpening applied, but it's useful to be able to fine-tune the sharpening strength after the fact in most situations.

Tip: Reduce Opacity Before Sharpening. If you reduce the sharpening layer's opacity to, for example, 66% before sharpening, you can use the Layer Opacity slider in the Layers palette to increase or decrease the strength of the sharpening after it's been applied.

Luminosity Blending

One of the key benefits of sharpening on a layer is that you can set the layer's blending mode to Luminosity, thereby avoiding the possibility of sharpening-induced hue shifts.

Some Photoshop gurus recommend converting images to Lab mode, sharpening the Lightness channel, then converting back to RGB. However, unless the image actually requires some other operation that demands Lab mode, roundtripping from RGB to Lab to RGB is a somewhat destructive process on 8-bit/channel images (you lose anywhere from 20 to 35 of the 256 levels available due to quantization error) that can lead to unwanted hue shifts and possible posterization. On 16-bit/channel images, the quantization error is a non-issue, but the conversion to Lab and back is time-consuming and may force you to flatten the image.

Applying sharpening with the Luminosity blend mode produces results that, while not identical to converting to Lab then sharpening the Lightness channel, still provide the main benefit of doing so—the sharpening changes only luminosity, not hue or saturation. (I'll discuss other ways of applying sharpening with Luminosity blend that don't depend on layers later in this chapter.)

Layer Masks

Another benefit to applying sharpening on a layer is that you can use a layer mask to localize the sharpening to specific areas of the image. I use layer masks with sharpening layers in two distinct ways:

▶ Edge masks localize sharpening along the edges in the image, protecting textured and flat areas from being sharpened.

▶ Brush masks let me paint sharpening in (and out) by painting on the layer mask with white or black.

Edge masks. Creating an edge mask is a multi-step process. The first step is to create a new channel that has good contrast along the edges you want to sharpen. In many cases, you can simply duplicate the red or green channel (the blue channel usually has more noise, and hence isn't a good candidate). If none of the existing channels works particularly well, try using Calculations (found on the Image menu) to produce a new channel with the desired contrast.

Calculations lets you combine two channels in all sorts of interesting ways. Figure 4-22 shows the Calculations dialog box, and the channel it produced using the settings shown.

Figure 4-22
Calculations

With the settings shown above, Calculations produces the channel shown at far right from the image shown at near right.

If you have the time and inclination to tailor the settings for each image, by all means experiment with different options in the Calculations dialog box. Otherwise, blending the red and green channels of the sharpening layer using Calculations set to Pin Light blending does a good job on most images.

The next step is to isolate the edges in the channel created by Calculations using the Find Edges filter, which can be found on the Stylize submenu of the Filter menu. Running Find Edges on the channel created by Calculations produces the result shown in Figure 4-23, which starts to look like an edge mask.

Figure 4-23
Find Edges

Applying the Find Edges filter to the channel created in Figure 4-22 produces the result shown at right.

But it needs some additional work. The edges are black, and they need to be white for a sharpening mask (black edges are useful for a noise reduction mask). So the next step is to invert the mask by choosing Image> Adjustments>Invert, or pressing Command-I. This inverts the mask so that the edges to be sharpened are white, and the flat areas to be protected are black.

The next two steps are to soften the mask with Gaussian Blur, and adjust the contrast with Levels or Curves. Blurring the mask smooths the transition between sharpened and unsharpend areas so that it appears more natural, and also provides some control over the width of the sharpening haloes. The contrast adjustment controls the intensity of the edge sharpening—the closer to white the edges are, the more they get sharpened—and the degree to which the non-edges are protected—the closer to black, the more they're protected. Figure 4-24 shows the inverted mask before and after blurring and tonal edits.

Figure 4-24
Fine-tuning the
edge mask

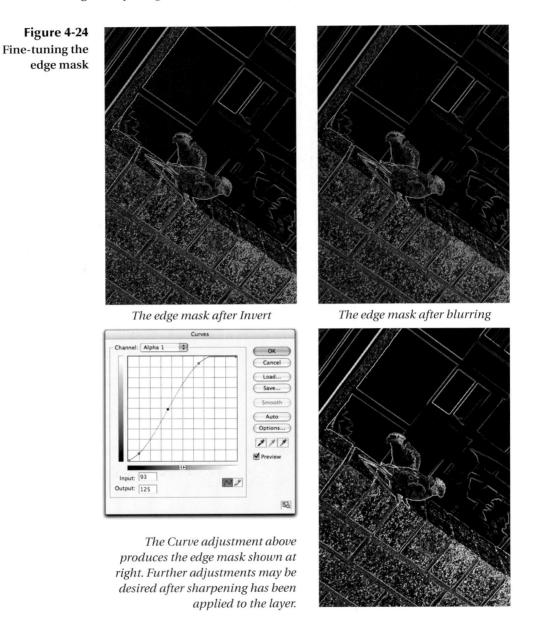

The edge mask after Invert

The edge mask after blurring

*The Curve adjustment above
produces the edge mask shown at
right. Further adjustments may be
desired after sharpening has been
applied to the layer.*

After the sharpening has been applied, you may wish to do further editing to the mask by blurring it, editing the contrast, or a combination of both. Before applying any sharpening, though, the final step is to add the mask channel to the sharpening layer as a layer mask. Figure 4-25 shows two ways of doing so. See the sidebar, "Selections, Channels, and Masks" for more information on working with masks.

Figure 4-25
Loading the edge mask
as a layer mask

Choose Load Selection
from the Select menu.

Choose the edge
mask channel
from the
Channel menu
in the Load
Selection
dialog box.

Make sure the
sharpening layer
is selected in the
Layers palette.

Choose Layer Mask>
Reveal Selection
from the Layer
menu.

The edge mask
is added to the
sharpening layer.

Or, Command-click the
edge mask channel's tile
in the Channels palette
to load the channel as a
selection.

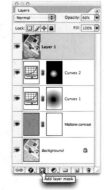

With the sharpening layer selected,
click the Add Layer Mask button in the
Layers palette.

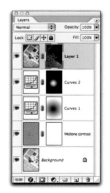

The edge mask
is added to the
sharpening layer.

Selections, Channels, and Masks

Selections, channels, and masks are all the same thing as far as Photoshop is concerned. They are simply three different roles played by the same data.

A selection is simply a temporary channel, which can be made permanent by saving it using the Save Selection command from the Select menu.

Saved Channels appear in the Channels palette. To load a channel as a selection, you can choose Load Selection from the Select menu, then choose the channel in the Load Selection dialog box. Or you can do so much more quickly by Command-clicking on the channel's tile in the Channels palette.

To add a channel as a layer mask, you must first load it as a selection using either of the methods just described. Then you can add it as a layer mask by selecting the layer and either choosing one of the Layer Mask commands from the Layer menu, or clicking the Add Layer Mask button in the Layers palette.

Once you've added the layer mask, you can apply sharpening to the layer. The layer mask focuses the sharpening on the edges while protecting the non-edges, so you can apply somewhat more aggressive sharpening than you can without a layer mask. The layer mask also gives you considerable control after the sharpening has been applied.

▶ You can adjust the transition between sharpened and nonsharpened areas by adjusting the contrast of the layer mask.

▶ You can, within limits, adjust the width of the sharpening haloes by blurring, then adjusting the contrast, of the mask.

I'll discuss these techniques in detail, and their place in the sharpening workflow, in the next chapter, *Putting the Tools to Work*.

Sharpening Brushes. A second important use of layer masks applied to sharpening layers is to create sharpening brushes. The technique is in essence very simple: create a sharpening layer using the technique described earlier in this chapter in "Sharpening on a Layer," apply sharpening to the layer, then add a layer mask that hides the sharpening (either by choosing Layer>Layer Mask>Hide All, or by Option-clicking the Add Layer Mask button in the Layers palette).

You can then brush sharpening into the image by painting on the layer mask with white to reveal the sharpening. However, a couple of nuances make this technique much more powerful than if you simply sharpen a layer, add a mask, and start painting!

▶ Set the sharpening layer to a medium opacity such as 66 percent. That way, you can easily adjust the global strength of the sharpening up or down by increasing or decreasing the layer's opacity.

▶ Apply sharpening that's slightly stronger than you're likely to want, then use a brush with a low opacity—I usually start at around 30 percent opacity. That way you can sneak up on the desired degree of sharpening by building up brush strokes.

If you paint in more sharpening than you want, you can paint it out again by switching the Foreground and Background colors (the quick way is to press the X key, with no modifiers) so that you're painting black into the mask. Figure 4-26 shows the construction and use of a sharpening brush layer.

Figure 4-26
A sharpening brush

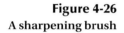

Create a sharpening layer set to Luminosity blending at 66 percent opacity.

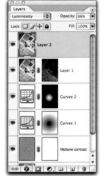

Apply sharpening.

Add a layer mask.

With the layer mask targeted in the Layers palette, paint with white using a low-opacity brush.

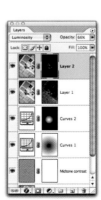

before brushing (200% zoom)

after brushing (200% zoom)

Of course, you can use this technique to brush *any* kind of adjustment into images—contrast, warming or cooling, and so on—but it's particularly useful for localized sharpening.

Smoothing brushes. A simple variant of this technique lets you create a smoothing brush by substituting Gaussian Blur for Unsharp Mask. (Adding about 2 percent of Gaussian monochromatic noise with the Add Noise filter makes the blur look less "digital" and more realistic.) You can brush in blurring as a way to soften skin textures, or you can knock back intrusive background details that detract from the subject—one way to make something appear sharper is to blur its surroundings.

Sharpening Tonal Ranges

Yet another benefit to sharpening on a layer is that you can constrain the sharpening to a specific tonal range. This is particularly useful in the early stages of the sharpening workflow, when it's essential to protect the extreme highlights and shadows so that there's enough headroom for final sharpening for output.

The key set of controls for doing so are the Blend If sliders in the Layer Style dialog box, which you can open by choosing one of the commands from the Layer Style submenu on the Layer menu, or, more conveniently, by double-clicking the layer's tile in the Layers palette. Note that you have to double-click on either the layer thumbnail or on the blank area to the right of the layer name—double-clicking the layer name simply makes the name editable! Figure 4-27 shows the Layer Style dialog box.

Figure 4-27
The Layer Style dialog box
and the Blend If sliders

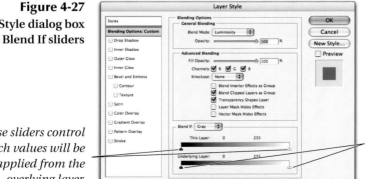

These sliders control which values will be applied from the overlying layer.

These sliders control which values in the underlying layer will accept values from the overlying layer.

The Blend If sliders are located at the bottom of the dialog box. The top slider controls which values in the overlying layer are applied to the image, while the bottom slider controls which values in the underlying layer(s) receive values from the overlying layer. Figure 4-28 shows the sliders in action.

Figure 4-28
The Blend If sliders
in action

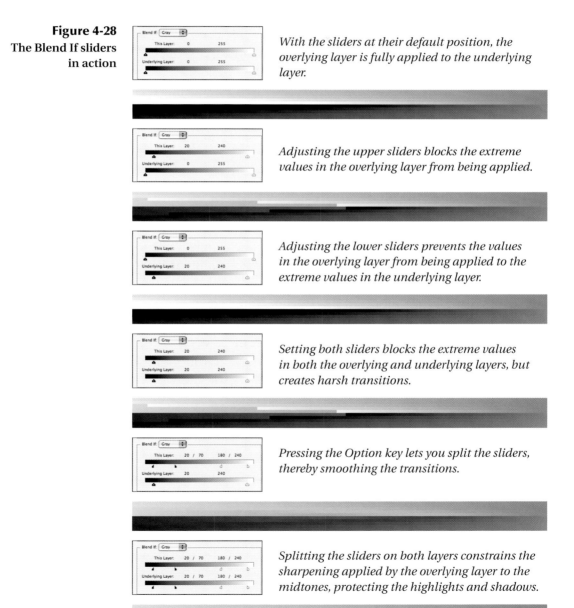

With the sliders at their default position, the overlying layer is fully applied to the underlying layer.

Adjusting the upper sliders blocks the extreme values in the overlying layer from being applied.

Adjusting the lower sliders prevents the values in the overlying layer from being applied to the extreme values in the underlying layer.

Setting both sliders blocks the extreme values in both the overlying and underlying layers, but creates harsh transitions.

Pressing the Option key lets you split the sliders, thereby smoothing the transitions.

Splitting the sliders on both layers constrains the sharpening applied by the overlying layer to the midtones, protecting the highlights and shadows.

Midtone sharpening. The Blend If sliders are the key to applying strong sharpening to the midtones while protecting the highlights and shadows. Using the sliders, it's possible to apply strong sharpening, yet confine it to the midtones, as shown in Figure 4-29.

Figure 4-29
Midtone sharpening

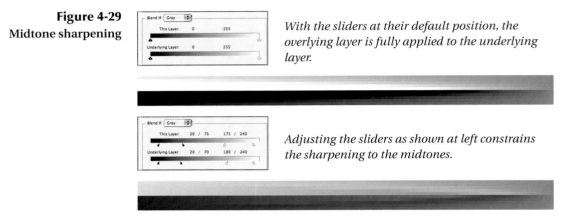

With the sliders at their default position, the overlying layer is fully applied to the underlying layer.

Adjusting the sliders as shown at left constrains the sharpening to the midtones.

I also use the Blend If sliders to apply midtone contrast, the lack of which is often confused with a lack of sharpness—see "Midtone Contrast," later in this chapter.

Sharpening Layer Controls

In practice, I often combine all the techniques discussed thus far on a single sharpening layer, starting with either a layer created by duplicating the Background layer on a flat file, or a new layer created by using Option-Merge Visible on a layered file.

I set the layer to Luminosity blending and 66 percent opacity. I set the Blend If sliders to apply sharpening only to the midtones, then I create an edge mask and apply it to the layer. Then I sharpen the layer. But I still have a significant amount of control after applying the sharpening.

▶ I can increase or decrease the global strength of the sharpening by adjusting the layer opacity up or down.

▶ I can adjust the strength of the sharpening along edges by editing the layer mask to lighten or darken the edges in the mask—the endpoint controls in Levels provide an easy way to do so.

► I can adjust the transition between sharpened and unsharpened areas by adjusting the contrast of the mask, using either Curves or the gray slider in Levels.

► I can adjust the width of the sharpening haloes by blurring the mask with Gaussian Blur, then editing with Levels or Curves to maintain the original tonality.

► I can fine-tune the tonal range to which the sharpening is applied by adjusting the Blend If sliders.

This type of layer-based sharpening lends itself well to automation using Actions. Most of the difficulties in doing so are a matter of taking into account the various assumptions and dependencies Actions always entail.

For example, when I record a sharpening layer Action, I always start by selecting the Background layer. Then I explicitly create a new layer, I use Option-Merge Visible to make the pixel content, and I use the menu command Layer>Arrange>Bring to Front to move the sharpening layer to the top of the layer stack.

I do this to make sure that the sharpening layer doesn't end up being created inside a layer group, which can easily happen if I don't take these steps. Note, however, that this technique creates its own dependency—the Action will fail on images that don't contain a Background layer.

One of the appealing aspects of automated sharpening layers that use these techniques is that they can be run as batch processes to make a large number of images good automatically, yet still provide enough control after sharpening to make the handful of hero images that justify handwork great rather than just good.

Overlay and High Pass

Another type of layer-based sharpening produces results that match traditional drum-scanner sharpening much more closely than anything Unsharp Mask or Smart Sharpen can achieve. This type of sharpening is produced by setting a duplicate layer created using Option-Merge Visible to Overlay blend mode, then running the High Pass filter. I do most of my final sharpening for print using this technique. The combination of an Overlay layer and the High Pass filter lends itself to two distinct techniques: sharpening, and adding midtone contrast.

Sharpening with Overlay and High Pass. This technique starts out with the creation of a sharpening layer, as described earlier in this chapter. The first point of departure, however, is that the layer is set to Overlay blending rather than Luminosity.

Overlay blending is essentially a contrast multiplier—when you set the layer to Overlay mode, you see a massive (and typically ugly) increase in contrast. The High Pass filter (found on the Filter>Other submenu) detects high-frequency transitions, and turns the rest of the layer gray, the neutral color for Overlay blend. The result is that the contrast boost is constrained to the high-frequency transitions, in other words, the edges. Figure 4-30 shows the Overlay/High Pass technique in action.

Figure 4-30
Sharpening with Overlay
and High Pass

The image before sharpening

The image after adding a sharpening layer set to Overlay, 66 percent opacity

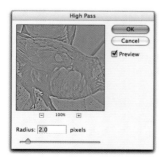

The High Pass Filter with Radius 2.0 pixels

The final result

The optimal Radius setting for High Pass varies with the image resolution and the output process—remember, the goal is to produce a sharpening halo that is too small to be distinguished as a separate feature at normal viewing distance—but typical settings for a sharpening effect are between 0.8 and 3 pixels. At higher Radius settings, Overlay and High Pass produce a contrast adjustment rather than sharpening. However, lack of midtone contrast is often perceived as a lack of sharpness.

Midtone contrast. Good midtone contrast is critical in conveying a sense of depth in an image, and one of the easiest ways to boost midtone contrast is to use an Overlay layer, the High Pass filter set to a high (30–50 pixel) Radius setting, and the Blend If sliders set to constrain the effect to the midtones.

I'm indebted to my friend and colleague Mac Holbert of Nash Editions for this particular variant of the technique. Some folks prefer to use Unsharp Mask with a high Radius and a low Amount in place of High Pass, while others favor Soft Light blending, which produces a gentler effect than Overlay. But the principle remains the same. Figure 4-31 shows how to boost midtone contrast.

Figure 4-31
Midtone contrast

This image is sharp, but it lacks midtone contrast.

The image with an Overlay layer set to 66 percent opacity.

Figure 4-31
Midtone contrast,
continued

*Running the High Pass filter
produces the result at right.
Setting the Blend If sliders to the
settings shown below produces
the final result, below right.*

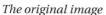
The original image

*The image after boosting midtone
contrast*

A great many images benefit enormously from a midtone contrast boost. This simple technique adds depth, and makes oversharpening less likely.

Sharpening and History

Layer-based sharpening offers great flexibility and control, but at the cost of greatly increased file sizes. In the next chapter, *Putting the Tools to Work*, I'll discuss some strategies for keeping file sizes manageable. In the meantime, here's a sharpening brush technique that doesn't rely on layers and masks. Instead, it uses Photoshop's History feature.

History offers much more than multiple Undo. It lets you blend multiple states of an image using the History Brush, or using the Fill command with a selection. The History palette is command central for working with History—see Figure 4-32.

Figure 4-32
The History palette

History sources

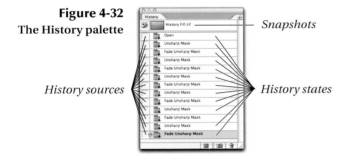

Snapshots

History states

Snapshots. You can save History states as Snapshots, which appear at the top of the History palette and aren't subject to the limit of the number of History states you set in Preferences>General, so they're always available until you close the document.

History states. History states accumulate on the History panel until they reach the limit specified in Preferences (the default is 20, I use 200), at which point the oldest History state gets dumped. You can switch between History states by clicking the state's tile in the History palette.

History sources. The column at the left of the History palette lets you specify a History state as the source for the History Brush, or for filling from History using the Fill command. Filling or brushing from History lets you blend one state of an image with another.

Fill from History. I use Fill from History when an easy selection is available, such as the example shown in Figure 4-33.

Figure 4-33
Fill from History

The original image

The image, right, after applying extreme sharpening, and the History palette, above, after doing so.

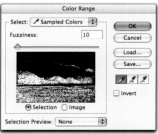

Making sure that Non-Linear History is enabled (choose History Options from the History palette menu and check the Allow Non-Linear History box), I click the original Open state in the History palette, and make a Color Range selection on the darker foreground hills, which I then feather by 10 pixels.

Figure 4-33
Fill from History, *continued*

I choose the final sharpening step (Fade Unsharp Mask) as my History source, then I choose Fill from the Edit menu, and specify From History, with Luminosity blending.

The image, right, after Fill from History

The final image, right, is produced by choosing Fade from the Edit menu, then fading the Fill to 50 percent opacity.

History Brush Sharpening. For more nuanced sharpening, I use the History Brush to brush sharpening into the image, as shown in Figure 4-34.

Figure 4-34
History Brush Sharpening

The original image

Figure 4-34
History Brush
Sharpening, *continued*

*I applied strong
sharpening by running
Unsharp Mask at five
different Radius settings,
and using the Fade
command after each
application of Unsharp
Mask to tone down the
effect to produce the
heavily oversharpened
result at right.*

The image after applying strong sharpening

Figure 4-34
History Brush
Sharpening, *continued*

*I returned the image
to its original state by
clicking the Open tile in
the History palette.*

*Then I selected the
final sharpening step as
the History Source, chose
the History brush set to
Luminosity mode with
a 33 percent opacity,
and painted the
sharpening selectively
into the image.*

The downside to using History to sharpen is that you have to get everything right in the current session, because once you close the document,
Photoshop forgets the history (so *you* are doomed to repeat it).

But sharpening with History offers almost as much control as sharpening with layers and masks. You can vary the brush opacity, you can Fade individual brush strokes (as long as you don't do anything else beforehand), or you can switch the History source to the unsharpened state to brush sharpening back out of the image.

If you're reasonably confident about what you're doing, sharpening with History creates smaller, simpler files than layer-based sharpening. You just don't have nearly as much freedom to change your mind after the fact.

Noise and Grain

Dealing with noise and grain is the opposite side of the coin from sharpening. Just as it's easy to overdo sharpening, it's also easy to overdo noise and grain removal, leading to two undesirable conditions.

► Overly aggressive noise removal produces soft, unnatural-looking images that scream "digital" and in extreme cases appear to have been run through the Median filter.

► Many noise reduction tools, including Photoshop's Reduce Noise filter, have a tendency to produce images that can't be sharpened, because as soon as you apply sharpening, artifacts from the noise removal pop into view.

In many cases, the best way to handle noise is to simply protect it from being sharpened, but in extreme cases—high-ISO or heavily underexposed digital captures, or scans from high-speed film, especially color negative—you may have to reduce the noise before you start sharpening.

It's worth noting that the market for third-party noise reduction plug-ins is one of the most competitive segments of the greater Photoshop plug-in market. If you routinely have to work with very noisy images, I suggest you consider one of the many third-party solutions available, because they almost all do a better job than can be achieved with Photoshop's tools.

But even the best third-party solutions are prone to producing the same kinds of artifacts as Photoshop's own Reduce Noise filter, though typically to a lesser extent, so the first key point about noise reduction is, don't overdo it! A somewhat noisy image is usually more palatable than one full of strange artifacts.

The Need for Noise Reduction

Remember that all the caveats about the size of sharpening haloes apply equally well to the size of noise artifacts. If the image is to be downsampled significantly, much of the noise may be downsampled out of existence.

Figure 4-35 shows a case in point. In the downsampled version of the image, the noise is unobtrusive because most of it was wiped out during downsampling, but the detail printed at 300 pixels per inch from the native-resolution file shows obvious, objectionable noise.

Figure 4-35
Noise and downsampling

In this downsampled version of the image, the noise is unobjectionable.

In this version of the image printed at native resolution, the noise is much more obvious.

Both versions of the image received identical sharpening for source and content, and both received identical output sharpening. The only difference is that the output sharpening was applied after downsampling to the downsampled version.

If your goal is to create a use-neutral master image, it makes sense to do the noise reduction on a separate layer, so that you can turn it off when it's not needed. If the image is for one-off use, consider carefully whether noise reduction is, in fact, needed.

Reduce Noise

Photoshop's Reduce Noise filter can do a creditable job, though it's frankly not as good as most third-party plug-ins. The danger with Reduce Noise is that you wind up creating an image that can't be sharpened. Figure 4-36 shows an example.

Figure 4-36
Reduce Noise dangers

This color negative scan is noisy.

Reduce Noise appears to eliminate most of the noise, but...

...sharpening brings the noise back, only with a regular rather than a random pattern, which is as bad as the original noise!

Reduce Noise with layers and masks. Reduce Noise is much more effective when used on a layer in conjunction with an edge mask. The technique for creating the layer and mask is essentially the same as that for a sharpening layer with an edge mask, only the edge mask for noise reduction isn't inverted, so the edges show as black and hence are protected from the noise reduction.

While it's tempting to simply invert the mask for noise reduction to use on a subsequent sharpening layer, you'll get better results, with less risk of unnatural transitions between sharpened and smoothed areas, if you do a little extra blurring and tone tweaking on the inverted mask before sharpening through it. Figure 4-37 shows the same image as Figure 4-36, with noise reduction and sharpening carried out through masks.

Figure 4-37
Reduce Noise and masks

Applying Reduce Noise through the mask at far right, with the settings shown below, produces the result at near right.

Noise reduction applied through a mask

The noise reduction mask

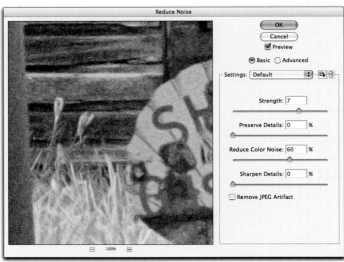

Figure 4-37
Reduce Noise and
masks, *continued*

Applying Unsharp Mask through the mask at far right, with the settings shown below, produces the result at near right.

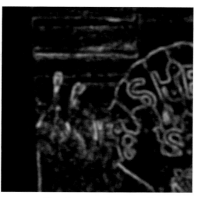

Sharpening applied through a mask

The sharpening mask

I created the sharpening layer using Option-Merge Visible.

I created the sharpening mask by duplicating the noise reduction mask, then applying a 1.3-pixel Gaussian Blur and a slight contrast boost.

The image at near right shows the noise reduction and the masked sharpening after sharpening for final output. The much noisier version at far right has identical sharpening but no noise reduction.

In this example, I've made the noise reduction quite strong, but still left some "tooth" in the image. The full-sized image at this resolution would be approximately 20 by 30 inches, so the viewing distance would likely be greater than the distance from which you're viewing this page.

Noise reduction always involves a trade-off between smoothness and sharpness. For less noise reduction, you can reduce the opacity of the noise reduction layer before performing the Option-Merge Visible step to create the sharpening layer.

Noise Reduction with Despeckle

The Despeckle filter is useful for dealing with mild-to-moderate luminance noise (as opposed to color noise). The secret is to apply Despeckle differentially to the three color channels—the red channel usually has the least noise, and the blue channel usually has the most.

Figure 4-38 shows the technique in action. It doesn't require the use of masks. When overdone, this technique can produce color shifts, but it provides an easy way of knocking back the worst of the noise.

Figure 4-38
Despeckle

This image has a good deal of luminance noise. It's even more obvious in the zoomed-in view, below right.

Figure 4-38
Despeckle, *continued*

The red channel

*The red channel
zoomed in*

*The red channel
after two applications of
the Despeckle filter*

Figure 4-38
Despeckle, *continued*

*The red channel zoomed
in after two applications
of the Despeckle filter*

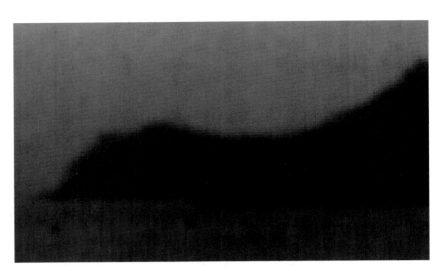

The green channel

*The green channel
zoomed in*

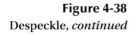

Figure 4-38
Despeckle, *continued*

*The green channel
after two applications of
the Despeckle filter*

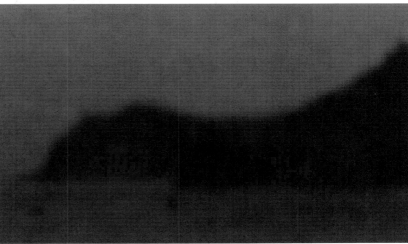

*The green channel
zoomed in after two
applications of the
Despeckle filter*

The blue channel

Figure 4-38
Despeckle, *continued*

*The blue channel
zoomed in*

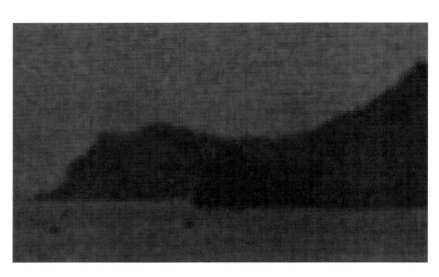

*The blue channel after
four applications of the
Despeckle filter*

*The blue channel
zoomed in after four
applications of the
Despeckle filter*

Figure 4-38
Despeckle, *continued*

The image with the despeckled layer at 66 percent opacity

The image zoomed in with the despeckled layer at 66 percent opacity

The image after final sharpening

Noise and the raw converter. The previous image was shot as JPEG. I also shot a raw version, and on the raw file I performed all the noise reduction in my raw converter of choice, Adobe Camera Raw. Unless the noise is extreme, I prefer to perform noise reduction on raw files in Camera Raw's Detail tab. Figure 4-39 shows the raw image before and after sharpening, with Luminance Smoothing set to 19 and Color Noise Reduction set to 15 in Camera Raw's Detail tab.

Figure 4-39
Camera Raw
noise reduction

The image with Camera Raw noise reduction, before sharpening

The image with Camera Raw noise reduction, after sharpening

If the noise is too extreme for the raw converter to handle, it's likely too extreme for any of Photoshop's built-in tools too.

Third-Party Solutions

In extreme noise situations, many third-party plug-ins do a better job than can be achieved using Photoshop's tools. ABSoft's Neat Image, Visual Infinity's Grain Surgery, PictureCode's Noise Ninja, and Imagenomic's Noiseware Professional all provide industrial-strength noise reduction with a great deal of control over the process. (If I've failed to mention your personal favorite, it's simply because the aforementioned plug-ins are the ones with which I'm most familiar.)

Here are a few general guidelines for using third-party noise reduction solutions:

▶ Always do noise reduction before sharpening. If you sharpen, you'll almost certainly make the noise worse; the noise reduction tool will have to work harder, and will probably wipe out the sharpening you did anyway.

▶ If you perform noise reduction on a layer, you can reduce the noise slightly more than you actually want, then fine-tune the noise reduction by tweaking the layer opacity.

▶ If you're working with raw images that are too noisy for the raw converter to handle, turn off all noise reduction in the raw converter and let the third-party tool handle all the noise. Otherwise the differing noise reduction algorithms in the raw converter and in the plug-in tend to fight one another.

▶ Don't overdo the noise reduction. A certain amount of noise is usually preferable to an image that looks like it's been blurred.

In practice, I find I need to resort to third-party tools only with high-ISO (800 or greater) or severely underexposed (more than 1 f-stop) digital captures, or with scans from color negative. In virtually all other situations, the techniques presented here work well.

Tools and Techniques

It should be clear after reading this chapter that knowing how a particular sharpening or smoothing tool works is only part of the answer. Learning to work with layers and masks provides you with much more control and flexibility than is attainable when you simply use the tools to burn changes into the pixels of a flattened image.

But as we all know, there's no such thing as a free lunch, and the downsides of doing everything on layers are that the files become very large, and also very complex. If you plan to leave the layers intact for maximum flexibility, *name them* in a way that you know will make sense to you several years hence. Otherwise you'll find yourself spending considerable amounts of time just figuring out what each layer does when you come to revisit the image.

In the next chapter, *Putting the Tools to Work*, I'll show you how to assemble the techniques covered in this chapter into a compete start-to-finish sharpening workflow.

Putting the Tools to Work

Building a Sharpening Workflow

In the last chapter, I covered a large body of sharpening and noise reduction techniques. In this chapter, I'll show you how to put the techniques together to make a complete sharpening workflow. The primary goal of the sharpening workflow is, of course, optimally sharpened images, but other benefits accrue too.

▶ Images that have been optimized for source and content become "use-neutral" master images that can easily be resampled and sharpened for multiple outputs.

▶ Much of the workflow can be automated (though creative localized sharpening cannot). An automated sharpening workflow can help you make hundreds of images good, so that you can reserve the manual work for the smaller number that need to be made great.

Sharpening on layers does, however, create very large files, so I'll also discuss when to apply sharpening layers in the workflow, and when it's safe to flatten them. Last but not least, I'll show you how to use Photoshop's actions to automate as much or as little of the sharpening process as you wish. In these days of digital capture, we have to process a great deal more data than we did when film was king, and actions are a key survival strategy if we want to avoid drowning in data!

When Do We Sharpen?

The sharpening workflow uses three sharpening passes, one of which, creative localized sharpening, is optional.

▶ Optimization for source and content can generally be achieved in a single operation. I recommend carrying out this phase as soon as all major corrections for tone and color have been done. Large moves in tone or color can increase noise, and distort or even wipe out sharpening, so the image should be close to final tonality before the initial sharpening.

In particular, if you plan to use the midtone contrast boost I described in the previous chapter (see "Midtone Contrast" in Chapter 4, *Sharpening Tools and Techniques*), I strongly recommend you do so before applying sharpening, because midtone contrast has a major impact on perceived sharpness, and can also exaggerate noise.

▶ Optional creative sharpening can be done at any time after the initial optimizations for source and content have been carried out, but should be done at the image's native resolution prior to any resampling for output.

▶ Sharpening for output should be done after any resampling to final ouput resolution. I do output sharpening as the last step prior to the color space conversion to output space.

When I print directly from Photoshop, I never actually convert the image to output space, letting Photoshop carry out the conversion on the print stream instead. When I deliver CMYK files for press, I sharpen as the final step prior to CMYK conversion. If final output size isn't known, I skip output sharpening, because the prepress operators will almost certainly sharpen the image after resampling. The images still benefit from the previous optimizations even if the prepress sharpening isn't absolutely optimal.

However, sharpening can have an impact on tonality, so don't be afraid to make fine-tuning adjustments to tone and color after applying source, content, or creative sharpening. Images that are well sharpened for output more often than not look hideous on screen, and my advice is to simply ignore the screen appearance.

Evaluating the Image

The first step is to decide what kind of optimization the image requires for both source and content. Source optimization for a specific digital camera is essentially constant, though at high ISO or on severely underexposed shots some noise reduction may be needed first. Source optimization for film scans depends on the scanner, the resolution at which the film is scanned, and the film format itself.

For digital captures, the goal of source optimization is to counteract the effect of the antialiasing filter, while with film scans, the focus may be more on noise reduction, especially with 35mm format.

Tip: Scanning to Reduce Noise. Some scanner drivers let you scan the film multiple times to reduce scanner noise. You can often get a much cleaner scan using four passes than you can using one. Some scanner drivers let you scan as many as 16 passes, which in my view is overkill. This technique suppresses scanner noise, but doesn't address film grain. A technique that does address film grain is to scan at a higher resolution than is needed, then downsample—this mitigates both scanner noise and film grain.

Next, you need to decide whether you want to treat the image as low-frequency, high-frequency, or something in between. Most images have both low-frequency and high-frequency components, but there's usually a dominant tendency you wish to emphasize—see "Optimizing for Image Content" in Chapter 3, *Sharpening Strategies*.

With source and content in mind, let's look at some real examples of optimizing for source and content, and the techniques used to do so.

Initial Optimization

I optimize for both source and content in a single process, because once the optimizations are done I can flatten the image to keep file sizes under control. With digital capture and larger-format film scans, you can use the same sharpening layer to optimize for both source and content. With 35mm film, or with high-speed medium- and large-format film, you may need to apply noise reduction as well as sharpening.

Source Optimization for Digital Capture

The goal in source optimization is to counteract the softening effects of the demosaicing process, and when present, the antialiasing filter. I do this using a sharpening layer set to Luminosity blending, with the Blend If sliders set to protect the highlights and shadows, concentrating the sharpening on the midtones. The sharpening Radius setting depends on the megapixel count of the camera, while the sharpening Amount depends on the strength of the antialiasing filter.

Creating a sharpening layer. The process starts with the creation of a sharpening layer, which is a simple, but detailed, process:

▶ Create a new layer by clicking the New Layer icon on the Layers palette, or by choosing New>Layer from the Layer menu.

▶ Press Option while choosing Merge Visible from the Layer menu, or press Command-Option-Shift-E.

▶ Set the newly created layer to Luminosity blend mode, 66 percent opacity.

▶ Double-click the layer's tile in the Layers palette to open the Layer Style dialog box, then set the Blend If sliders to the settings shown in Figure 5-1.

Note that these Blend If settings are optimized for the gamma 1.8 tone curve of my preferred Photoshop working space, ProPhoto RGB. If you prefer a gamma 2.2 space such as Adobe RGB, try Black Minimum 20, Black Maximum 80, White Minimum 145, White Maximum 235 instead.

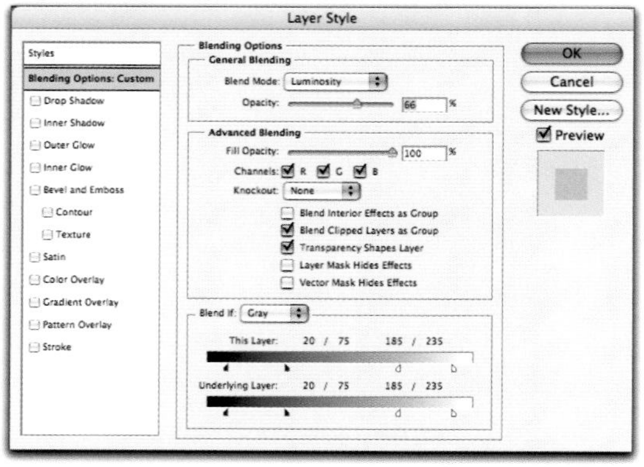

Figure 5-1
Blend If settings for
sharpening layer

Set the Blend If sliders
for both layers to Black
Minimum 20, Black
Maximum 75, White
Minimum 185, White
Maximum 235.

Automating the sharpening layer. Repetitive and fiddly tasks such as creating a sharpening layer cry out for automation! You can make a simple action to create the sharpening layer as follows.

▶ In the Actions palette, create a new Action set by clicking the New Set button in the Actions palette, then, in the ensuing dialog box, name the set "Sharpening." The new set appears at the bottom of the Actions palette—see Figure 5-2.

Figure 5-2
Create an action set

Click the New set button to create a new set.

The new set appears at the bottom of the Actions palette.

Name it "Sharpening."

▶ Click the New Action button in the Actions palette, name the action "Sharpening Layer" in the ensuing dialog box, then click Record—see Figure 5-3.

Figure 5-3
Create an action

Click the New Action button to create a new action.

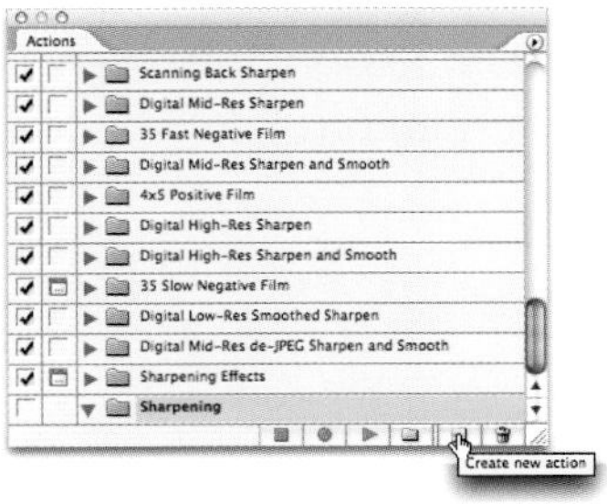

Name it "Sharpening Layer," then click Record.

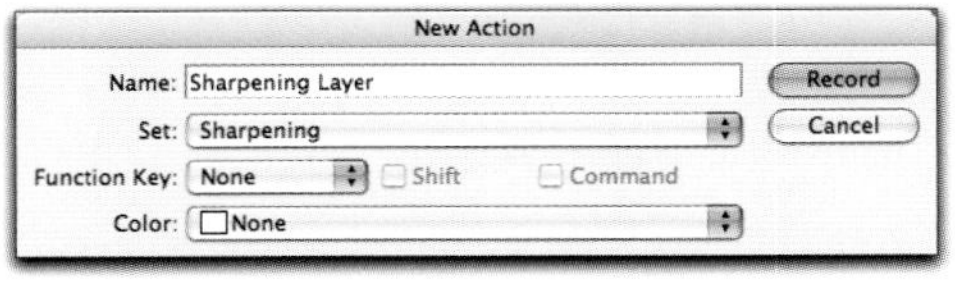

▶ Click the New Layer button in the Layers palette to add a new layer, then press Command-Option-Shift-E (or hold down Option while choosing Merge Visible from the Layer menu) to fill the new layer with a merged copy of the image—see Figure 5-4.

Figure 5-4
Add a new layer.

Click the New Layer button in the Layers palette to add a new layer, then press Command-Option-Shift-E.

▶ Double-click the new layer's tile in the Layers palette to open the Layer Styles dialog box, then set the blend mode to Luminosity, the opacity to 66 percent, and both Blend If sliders to Black Minimum 20, Black Maximum 75, White Mimimum 185, White Maximum 235, and click OK to close the dialog box—see Figure 5-5.

Figure 5-5
Set blend mode, opacity and Blend If sliders.

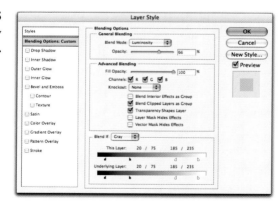

Set the blend mode to Luminosity and the layer opacity to 66%, then set the Blend If sliders for both layers to Black Minimum 20, Black Maximum 75, White Minimum 185, White Maximum 235.

▶ Choose Layer>Arrange>Bring to Front or press Command-Shift-] to move the new layer to the top of the layer stack. Last but not least, double-click the new layer's name in the Layers palette to make it editable, then name it with a name you'll understand (I use "Presharpen") and click the Stop button in the Actions palette to stop recording—see Figure 5-6.

Figure 5-6
Complete the action.

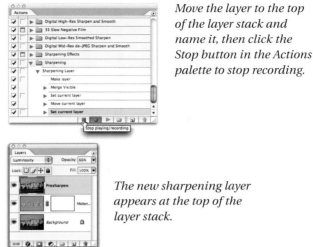

Move the layer to the top of the layer stack and name it, then click the Stop button in the Actions palette to stop recording.

The new sharpening layer appears at the top of the layer stack.

Now you can use the action you just created to add a sharpening layer to any image. Note, however, that this action will fail if you run it when the currently selected layer is inside an open layer group—the sharpening layer will appear as the top layer in the group rather than as the top layer in the stack. All the workarounds I know create other dependencies, and you can easily work around this one by dragging the layer out of the group and placing it at the top of the stack if necessary.

Note too that you can't simply record dragging the layer to the top of the stack: doing so records the relative position of the layer in the document at hand rather than the absolute, top-of-the-stack position. You must use Layer>Arrange>Bring to Front, or its keyboard shortcut.

Sharpening for image source. Source optimization for most digital captures can be done with a single application of Unsharp Mask, tuned to the camera's sensor. The Radius setting is related to the megapixel count of the sensor, while the Amount is determined by the amount of antialiasing in the camera's optics.

Since the layer is constrained by both the Blend If sliders and the layer opacity controls, you can apply surprisingly strong doses of Unsharp Mask during this first phase of sharpening. One difference between film and digital is that with the former, the ability to resolve fine detail degrades gradually, while with the latter, there's a fairly sharp cutoff. You want to set the Radius to the smallest value that still reveals detail. Figure 5-7 shows images from two 6-megapixel cameras.

While both cameras capture 6 megapixels, the Kodak DCS 460, which lacks an antialiasing filter, produces a considerably sharper image than the Canon EOS 300D, which contains a fairly aggressive antialiasing filter. So the image from the Canon camera both requires and can tolerate a much stronger sharpening at this stage than can the Kodak camera.

Since both cameras are 6-megapixel cameras, they both take the same Radius setting of 0.6 pixels—a higher Radius starts to block fine detail and a lower one fails to reveal any additional detail. Table 5-1 shows suggested Radius settings for different-density sensors. If you're lucky enough to work with a very high megapixel camera, you may want to try an even

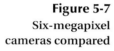

Figure 5-7
Six-megapixel
cameras compared

*The image at right and
the detail below right
were shot with a
6-megapixel Kodak
DCS 460.*

	Megapixel count	Sharpening Radius
Table 5-1 **Megapixels and Radius**	≤ 4 megapixels	1 pixel
	6 megapixels	0.6 pixel
	8 megapixels	0.5 pixel
	≥ 11 megapixels	0.4 pixel

smaller radius, but the effect of Radius 0.3 is dramatically weaker than that of Radius 0.4. Figure 5-8 shows the same image details after sharpening for source. The Canon camera received a much stronger correction, but the two images have approximately the same apparent sharpness.

Figure 5-7
Six-megapixel
cameras compared,
continued

The image at right and the detail below right were shot with a 6-megapixel Canon EOS 300D.

Figure 5-8
Six-megapixel
cameras sharpened
for source

*The Kodak DCS 460
image at right was
sharpened with Radius
0.6, Amount 210.*

*The Canon EOS 300D
image at right was
sharpened with Radius
0.6, Amount 500.*

Both images will require further sharpening, but this first sharpening step removes a good deal of softness and helps produce a better layer mask to use in the subsequent sharpening steps.

Source Optimization for Film Scans

It's quite a bit harder to make generalizations about film scans than about digital capture because more variables are involved—the scanner, the scan resolution, the film speed, and the film format all make their contributions. The goal, however, is always to improve the relationship between the detail we want to sharpen and the noise we want to mitigate or eliminate.

As a result, source optimization for film may use a sharpening layer just like source optimization for digital captures, or it may entail prior use of a noise reduction layer before sharpening.

The need for noise reduction. Most film scans can benefit from some degree of noise reduction. The exceptions are relatively low-resolution scans of medium- and large-format film, where the scanner hasn't yet begun to detect grain. Bear in mind that grain shows up in scans at much lower resolutions than are required to resolve the grain.

Film scans from 35mm format almost always benefit from some noise reduction, unless the scans are very low-resolution. With larger formats, negatives are more likely to demand noise reduction than positives, because the noise is exaggerated when the very narrow dynamic range of the film is edited to provide a full-range image, and higher-resolution scans may benefit from noise reduction more than lower-resolution ones simply because they reveal more of the grain.

The best rule of thumb I can offer is, if sharpening through a sharpening layer makes the grain significantly more obvious, the image is a good candidate for noise reduction before sharpening!

Gentle noise reduction and sharpening. For mild noise reduction followed by sharpening for source, I use a normal layer created by using Option-Merge Visible, and a mild application of the Reduce Noise filter. Then I create a sharpening layer using the same techniques I use for digital capture.

Figure 5-9 shows a high-resolution scan from 4x5 transparency film. It has relatively little noise, but still benefits from a mild round of noise reduction before sharpening for source. I prefer to perform noise reduction and sharpening on separate layers, because I may fine-tune the opacity of the noise reduction layer after doing the sharpening, but the resulting files do get very large.

If file size is a critical concern, you can trade a modest amount of control for a substantially smaller file by flattening the image after applying noise reduction. What you *don't* want to do is to sharpen the noise reduction layer, because the Luminosity blend mode and the Blend If sliders are critical for source sharpening, but don't work well for noise reduction (and in fact don't work at all for color noise reduction). I'll point out other opportunities for reducing file size later in the workflow.

Figure 5-9   Source optimization with gentle noise reduction

The entire image

A 300-ppi detail

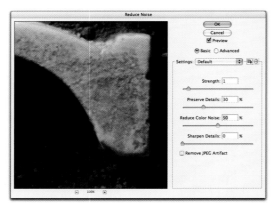

Running the Reduce Noise filter on a layer created using Option-Merge Visible, set to Normal blend with 100 percent opacity, produces the result shown at right. The effect is almost imperceptible, but it makes a difference to the subsequent sharpening layer.

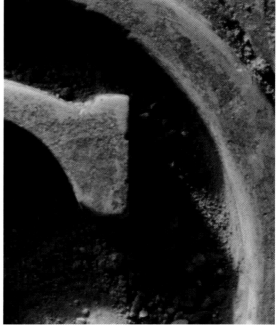

Figure 5-9   Source optimization with gentle noise reduction

Running the Unsharp Mask filter with the settings shown above, on a layer created using the sharpening layer action described earlier in this chapter, produces the result at right.

The image at right shows the result of applying the Unsharp Mask filter to the sharpening layer without first carrying out the noise reduction. The difference is subtle, but this version of the image won't take further sharpening as well as the one that had noise reduction applied.

The effect of the noise reduction layer is quite subtle, but it makes the image much more able to withstand subsequent sharpening. Reduce Noise works well at mild settings such as the ones used on this image, and the sharpened version shows no trace of any artifacts created by the noise reduction process. I'm indebted to my friend and colleague Jeff Schewe for this image.

Moderate noise reduction and sharpening. Figure 5-10 shows a scan from a 35mm transparency that requires stronger noise reduction than the previous example. The stronger grain of 35mm requires stronger Reduce Noise settings which soften the image noticeably, so I mitigate the effect by adding a layer mask to the Reduce Noise layer that protects the edges.

Figure 5-10
Reduce Noise on
a masked layer

The entire image

A 300-ppi detail

Figure 5-10
Reduce Noise on
a masked layer,
continued

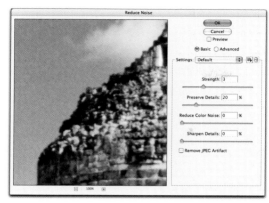

Running the Reduce
Noise filter with Strength
3, Preserve Details 20,
and all other settings
at 0 produces the result
shown below.

After Reduce Noise

I created this layer
mask by running
Calculations with the
Noise Reduction layer
selected, blending the
Red and Blue channels
with Pin Light. I then
ran the Find Edges filter,
applied a 5-pixel
Gaussian Blur, and
adjusted the white Input
slider in Levels to 240.

Figure 5-10
Reduce Noise on
a masked layer,
continued

*The Reduce Noise layer
after adding the
layer mask*

*The image after adding
a sharpening layer and
running Unsharp Mask
with Amount 200 and
Radius 0.8*

The addition of the edge mask to the noise reduction layer lets me apply enough noise reduction to reduce the grain in the sky without softening the important edges in the image too much. The addition of the sharpening layer essentially returns the image to its original sharpness, but with less grain.

Strong noise reduction with Despeckle. Figure 5-11 shows a 35mm color negative scan, which has the typical strong grain of scanned color neg. The Reduce Noise filter simply isn't strong enough to handle this kind of film grain (or rather, it creates unsharpenable images when the strength is turned up high enough to do so). Instead, I use the Despeckle filter.

Figure 5-11   Source optimization with strong noise reduction

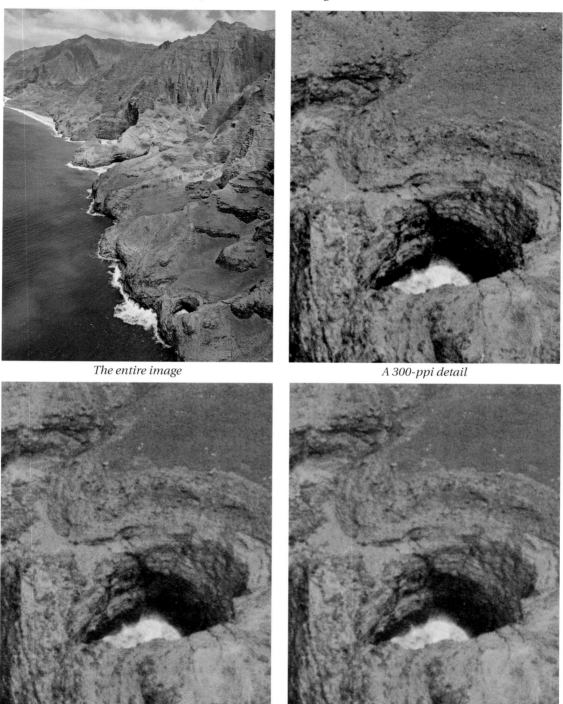

The entire image

A 300-ppi detail

The red channel

The red channel after Despeckle once

Figure 5-11 Source optimization with strong noise reduction, *continued*

The green channel

The green channel after Despeckle twice

The blue channel

The blue channel after Despeckle four times

Figure 5-11   Source optimization with strong noise reduction, *continued*

After channel-specific Despeckle   *After Unsharp Mask Amount 200, Radius 1.2*

The key to using Despeckle for aggressive noise reduction is to use it as little as possible, which means running it differentially on each channel. In the example in Figure 5-11, I ran Despeckle once on the red channel, twice on the green channel, and four times on the blue channel.

I then completed the source optimization by creating a sharpening layer using the action previously described in this chapter, and running Unsharp Mask on that layer with Amount at 200, Radius at 1.2, and Threshold at 0. The result is that the image has approximately the original sharpness but with a lot less grain.

Automating source optimization. You can extend the sharpening layer action I described earlier to cover the entire task of optimizing for image source (and, as you'll see later in this chapter, for content too). You have a choice as to the basic strategy, however:

▶ You can create multiple actions with different preset settings, or

▶ You can insert stops in a single action at the various decision points.

The choice is up to you. If you want to hand-tune every single image, inserting stops is a good way to go. If you need to batch-process hundreds or thousands of images, presets make more sense.

Automating noise reduction #1. Here's an action for creating a noise reduction layer and applying the Reduce Noise filter.

▶ In the Actions palette, select the Sharpening set created in the previous action described earlier in this chapter, then click the New Action button in the Actions palette. Name the action "Noise Reduction" in the ensuing dialog box, then click Record—see Figure 5-12.

Figure 5-12
Create the Noise
Reduction action.

Click the New Action button to create a new action.

Name it "Noise Reduction," then press Record.

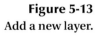

▶ Click the New Layer button in the Layers palette to add a new layer, then press Command-Option-Shift-E (or hold down Option while choosing Merge Visible from the Layer menu) to fill the new layer with a merged copy of the image—see Figure 5-13.

Figure 5-13
Add a new layer.

Click the New Layer button in the Layers palette to add a new layer, then press Command-Option-Shift-E.

▶ Choose Layer>Arrange>Bring to Front or press Command-Shift-] to move the new layer to the top of the layer stack. Last but not least, double-click the new layer's name in the Layers palette to make it editable, then name it (I use "Reduce Noise").

▶ Run the Reduce Noise filter using your desired settings, then click the Stop button in the Actions palette to stop recording. To handle different Reduce Noise settings, you can either duplicate the action and re-record the Reduce Noise step (which you can do quickly by Option-double-clicking on that step in the action), or turn on the dialog box for this step, which will make the action open the Reduce Noise dialog box for user input—see Figure 5-14.

Figure 5-14
Varying the
Reduce Noise step

Duplicate the action, then Option-double-click the Reduce Noise step to record it again with new settings, or...

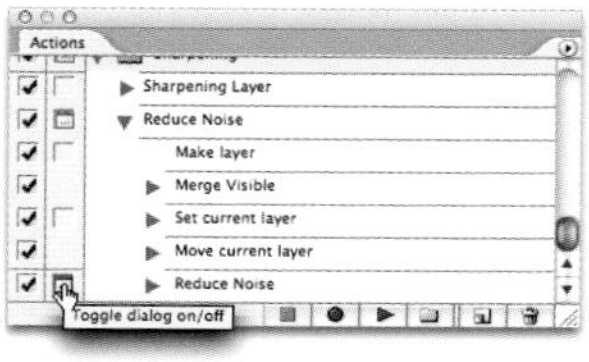

...click in the Toggle Dialog column to make the Reduce Noise dialog box appear when the action is run.

Automating noise reduction #2. This action extends the previous one by adding a layer mask to the Reduce Noise layer. The goal of the layer mask is to make the noise reduction apply less to the edges than to the non-edges, not to block it completely, so the layer mask won't contain any solid black pixels.

▶ Follow the steps for the previous action all the way through running Reduce Noise, but instead of stopping afterwards, choose Calculations from the Image menu. Set the layer for both Source 1 and Source 2 to Reduce Noise, set the Channel for Source 1 to Red and Source 2 to Green, and the Blending to Pin Light to create a new channel—see Figure 5-15.

Figure 5-15
Create a new channel
with Calculations.

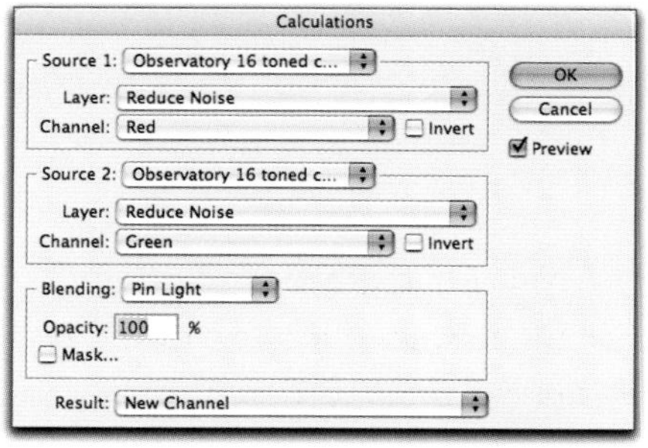

Blend the red and green channels using Pin Light to create a new channel that forms the basis of the layer mask.

► Run the Find Edges filter, then apply Gaussian Blur with a 3-to-5-pixel Radius. The Radius setting depends on the scan resolution, with the lower value for low-resolution scans and the higher one for high-resolution scans—see Figure 5-16.

Figure 5-16
Find Edges and
Gaussian Blur

After running Find Edges, apply a Gaussian Blur of 3–5 pixels, depending on the scan resolution.

► Use the Curves command to apply a two-point Curves adjustment with the first point at input 0, output 50 and the second point at input 195, output 230—see Figure 5-17.

Figure 5-17
Lighten the mask with
a Curves adjustment.

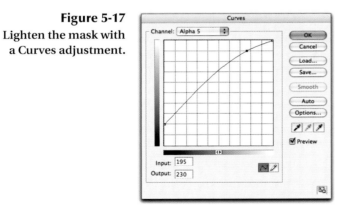

Lighten the mask channel with a two-point Curves adjustment.

► Command-click the channel's thumbnail in the Channels palette, or click the Load Selection button at the bottom of the Channels palette, to load the channel as a selection—see Figure 5-18.

Figure 5-18
Load the channel
as a selection.

Channel thumbnail ———————————— *Load Selection button*

▶ Click the Add layer mask button in the Layers palette to add the channel to the Reduce Noise layer as a layer mask, then click the Stop button in the Actions palette to stop recording—see Figure 5-19.

Figure 5-19
Load the selection
as a layer mask.

*Click the Add
layer mask button*

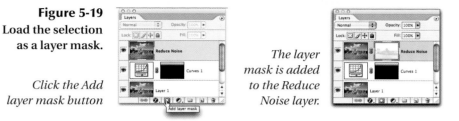

*The layer
mask is added
to the Reduce
Noise layer.*

If you deal with a single scanner and film format, a single action should take care of the noise reduction duties. If you deal with different film formats or different scan resolutions, you can either duplicate the action and rerecord the Gaussian Blur and, optionally, the Curves adjustment steps, or you can toggle the dialog boxes on for these steps—see Figure 5-20.

Figure 5-20
Customize the action

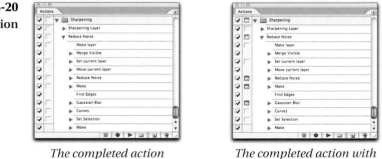

The completed action   *The completed action with
dialogs turned on*

Automating noise reduction #3. For heavy noise, such as color negative grain, the Reduce Noise filter simply doesn't do the job. Instead, I rely on the Despeckle filter. The following action runs Despeckle once on the red channel, twice on the green channel, and four times on the blue channel, which usually provides enough noise reduction.

▶ Duplicate the previous action steps up to the point where you're ready to run the Reduce Noise filter (you may want to give the layer a different name, such as "Reduce Strong Noise"), then click Record and run the Despeckle filter instead. It applies to all three channels.

▶ Select the green channel by clicking its tile in the channels palette, and run the Despeckle filter once more. The green channel has now had Despeckle applied twice.

▶ Select the blue channel and run the Despeckle filter three times, so that the blue channel has been despeckled a total of four times, then click the Stop button to stop recording.

There are two ways to combine this action with the sharpening layer action described earlier in this chapter. You can copy the steps from the sharpening layer action into any or all of the noise reduction actions, or you can record an action that plays the previously recorded actions. If you opt for the latter route, it's a good idea to make sure that any action that calls other actions is saved in the same Action set as the actions it's calling; otherwise, if the called actions aren't available, it will fail. See Figure 5-21.

Figure 5-21
Combining actions

Shift-click to select all the action steps you want to copy, then Option-drag them to the desired location (in this case, the end of the Reduce Noise action).

The selected steps are copied to the action.

Alternatively, create a new action, start recording, and play the first action, then the second, then click Stop.

To complete the source optimization automation, you can record an action step that applies Unsharp Mask to the sharpening layer, either appended to the end of the sharpening layer action, or as a separate action that other actions can call.

Optimizing for Image Content

Once the source optimization is completed, the next step in the workflow is to optimize for image content. See "Sharpening and Image Content" in Chapter 2, *Why Do We Sharpen?* for a discussion of the differing requirements imposed by image content. In this section, I'll concentrate on the process.

For all image types, the process is the same. We start by creating a layer mask that protects the non-edges and exposes the edges to editing, we apply that layer mask to the sharpening layer we used to optimize for source, and then we apply additional sharpening to that masked layer. The control points are the degree of blurring applied to the mask, and the sharpening settings used.

In this section, I'll show you typical optimizations for a high-frequency image, a mid-frequency image, and a low-frequency image. For any given image source, I find that it works quite well to treat all images as either low-, mid-, or high-frequency, but if you want more nuanced manual treatments, you can make the mask blurring and layer sharpening adjustments by hand on each image, trading more control for more work.

Content Optimization, Low-Frequency

The image in Figure 5-22 contains mid-frequency and high-frequency components, but the general tendency is low-frequency: I want to sharpen the dominant features without emphasizing high-frequency detail like skin texture. I can accomplish this using the combination of a soft-edged mask and a fairly wide sharpening Radius.

The starting point is the sharpening layer used to optimize for the image source. It may seem a scary prospect to sharpen this layer again, but bear in mind that the combination of the layer's reduced opacity (66 percent), the effect of the Blend If sliders in forcing the sharpening into the mid-tones, and the effect of the layer mask attached to the sharpening layer all act together to make the sharpening quite mild.

Figure 5-22
A low-frequency image

In this low-frequency image, we want to sharpen the big features without emphasizing skin texture or other high-frequency detail.

Low-frequency edge mask. I've used several techniques in the past to create low-frequency edge masks, but the one that seems to work best in the greatest number of cases is to start out with a blurred copy. I make this by creating a layer using Option-Merge Visible, which I then blur with Gaussian Blur—see Figure 5-23.

Figure 5-23
Creating a blurred layer

*I create a new layer
using Option-Merge
Visible.*

*I apply a Gaussian Blur
with a 10-pixel Radius.*

To create the mask channel, I use Calculations, blending the Red and Green channels with Pin Light blend, and making sure that the blurred layer is selected for both sources—see Figure 5-24.

Figure 5-24
Creating the mask channel

*I create the new mask
channel at right by
running Calculations
on the blurred layer.*

Running Find Edges, then Levels, followed by Image>Adjustments>Invert creates a soft-edged mask—see Figure 5-25.

Figure 5-25
Making a soft edge mask

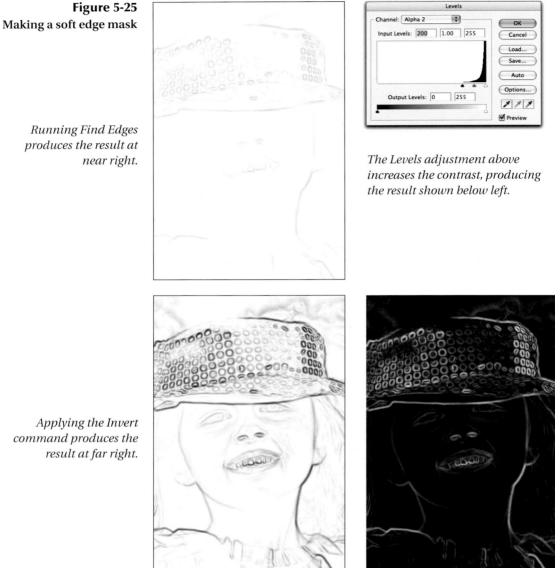

Running Find Edges produces the result at near right.

The Levels adjustment above increases the contrast, producing the result shown below left.

Applying the Invert command produces the result at far right.

The mask is almost finished. The extreme tonal edit has introduced some posterization in the midtones, which I soften using a second Gaussian Blur with a Radius of 10 pixels. Gaussian Blur makes more tonal values available and hence reduces posterization, but it also reduces the contrast, so I finish off the mask channel with another, gentler Levels adjustment—see Figure 5-26.

Figure 5-26
Fine-tuning the mask

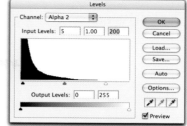

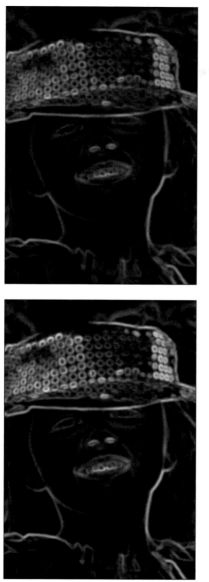

*Running a 10-pixel
Gaussian Blur produces
the result at near right.*

*The Levels adjustment above
increases the contrast, producing
the result shown below.*

The final mask channel

Loading the mask. With the mask channel completed, I can now load it as a selection, and add it to the sharpening layer as a layer mask. Once I've done so, I can delete both the blurred layer and the alpha channel, since they've served their purpose, to keep the file size down. If I need to retrieve the alpha channel, I can do so by targeting the sharpening layer—the layer mask then appears in the Channels palette. Figure 5-27 shows the steps for adding the layer mask and deleting the layer and the alpha channel.

Figure 5-27
Loading the mask

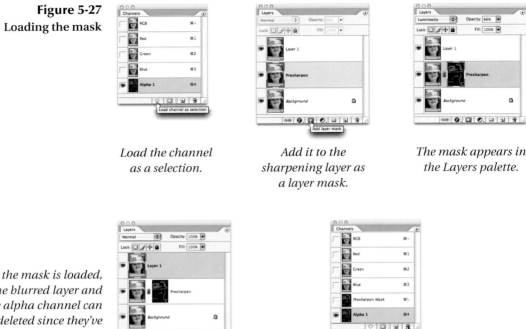

Load the channel
as a selection.

Add it to the
sharpening layer as
a layer mask.

The mask appears in
the Layers palette.

*Once the mask is loaded,
the blurred layer and
the alpha channel can
be deleted since they've
served their purpose.*

Final sharpening for content. With the mask in place, I can now apply the sharpening for content. Since I'm applying the sharpening to a masked layer with reduced opacity, I can apply strong sharpening and still obtain a very subtle result. Note that the proxy view in the Unsharp Mask filter ignores both the mask and the layer opacity, so it looks quite scary! Figure 5-28 shows the results of the final sharpening, with Unsharp Mask at Amount 180, Radius 3, Threshold 0.

Notice that the final optimization for source and content has less sharpening than the image optimized for source. That's an intended effect of the layer mask. The initial optimization for source simply makes the content optimization more effective—it's not designed as a global sharpen.

The variables in the content optimization are the values for the two rounds of Gaussian Blur, the first on the blurred layer, the second on the mask channel itself; and the settings for the final Unsharp Mask step. This example is an 8.2-megapixel digital capture. For smaller files, reduce the Radius settings slightly, and for larger ones, increase them. I'll discuss the numbers in more detail later in this chapter. First, to provide more context for that discussion, let's look at medium- and high-frequency images.

Figure 5-28
Final sharpening

The unsharpened image

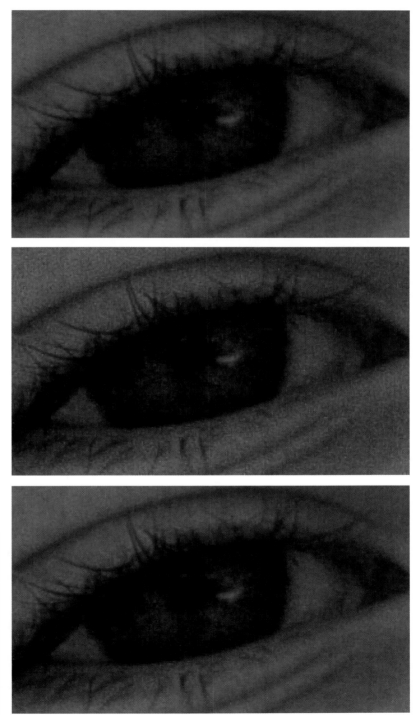

*The image sharpened
for source, right, and
sharpened for source
and content, below*

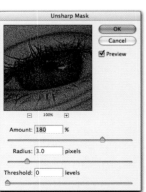

Content Optimization, Mid-Frequency

The optimization process for mid-frequency images is the same as for low-frequency ones: The only difference is the values used for the Gaussian Blurs and for the final sharpening. Again, we start with the sharpening layer created during the source optimization.

Figure 5-29 shows a mid-frequency image. It has low- and high-frequency components, but the dominant tendency I want to emphasize is the medium-frequency edges.

Figure 5-29
A mid-frequency image

For this type of image, I use a much smaller Radius setting for the Gaussian Blur I apply to make the blurred layer, and an even smaller Radius setting for the Gaussian Blur applied to the mask. The reason for using a blurred layer is to influence the behavior of the Find Edges filter.

If I don't build the layer mask from a blurred layer, Find Edges creates very narrow edges that produce a sharp transition between sharpened and unsharpened pixels. I can mitigate this to some extent by blurring the mask itself, but for low- and mid-frequency images, working from a blurred layer is more effective. Figure 5-30 shows the stages involved in creating the edge mask for this image.

Figure 5-30
Creating the edge mask

I start by creating a new layer with Option-Merge Visible. I apply a 1-pixel Gaussian Blur, then use Calculations to produce the channel shown below left.

Running the Find Edges filter on the channel shown at near right produces the result shown at far right.

Figure 5-30
Creating the edge mask,
continued

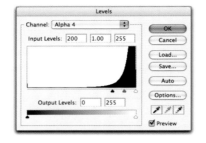

Running the Levels adjustment above, followed by Image>Adjustments>Invert, produces the result at right.

A 0.4-pixel Radius Gaussian Blur followed by the Levels adjustment at far right produces the final layer mask, below.

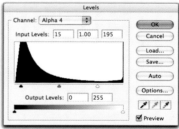

Once the mask channel is finalized, the procedure for adding it to the sharpening layer and deleting the blurred layer and the mask channel is identical to that for the low-frequency image. I can then apply the final sharpening for content by targeting the sharpening layer and running Unsharp Mask with Amount 200, Radius 0.8, Threshold 0. Figure 5-31 shows a detail from the image before and after optimization.

Figure 5-31
Mid-frequency
optimization

unsharpened   *optimized for source*

optimized for source and content

Content Optimization, High-Frequency

The procedure for sharpening a high-frequency image for content differs from that for low- and mid-frequency images in that there's no need to create a blurred layer. Instead, we simply blur the mask channel after running Find Edges. On some images, the mask may need tonal editing, but I prefer to wait until the sharpening has been applied before making that decision. Figure 5-32 shows a high-frequency image with lots of fine detail.

Figure 5-32
A high-frequency image

Making the mask. Creating the edge mask for this type of image is a simpler process than for low- or mid-frequency images. I use Calculations to create a new channel, but instead of creating a blurred layer from which to do so, I instead start with the sharpening layer used for source optimization. Once the new channel is created, I run Find Edges. I use Image>Adjustments>Invert to invert the channel, and run a small-radius (0.8-pixel) Gaussian Blur. Figure 5-33 shows the process.

Since the mask generated by this method has been blurred only very lightly, it still covers a full tonal range, so the Levels edits required in the previous two techniques are unnecessary. I may edit the layer mask after sharpening has been applied, though—see "Post-Sharpening Control," later in this chapter.

Adding the layer mask uses the same technique as the previous optimizations—load the channel as a selection, target the sharpening layer, add the mask, then sharpen. Figure 5-34 shows the result of the sharpening.

Figure 5-33
Creating the edge mask

Making sure that the Presharpen layer is set for both sources, I combine the red and green channels to create the new channel shown below.

The new channel created from Calculations

The new channel after running Find Edges

Figure 5-33
Creating the edge mask,
continued

*The new channel
inverted*

*Applying a 0.8-pixel
radius Gaussian Blur
produces the final mask,
below.*

The final mask

Figure 5-34
Before and after
sharpening

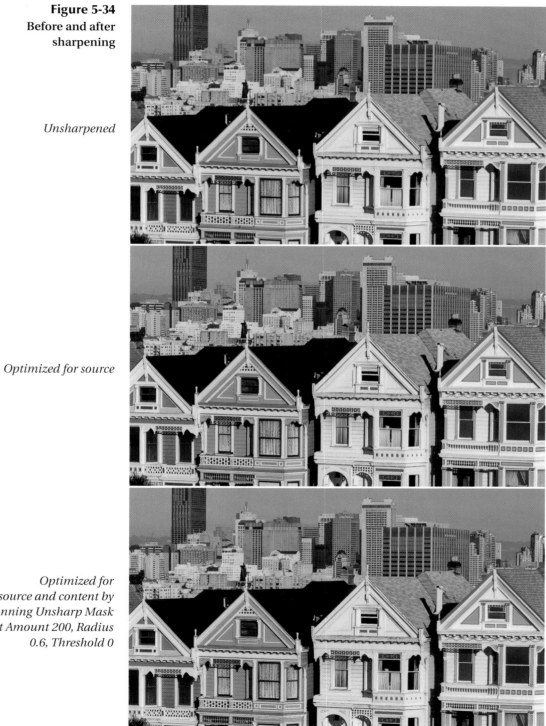

Unsharpened

Optimized for source

*Optimized for
source and content by
running Unsharp Mask
at Amount 200, Radius
0.6, Threshold 0*

Post-Sharpening Control

Once the sharpening (and when appropriate, noise reduction) layers have been applied, you still have considerable control over the sharpening. The first level of control is the layer opacity of the sharpening layer. Creating the layer with an opacity of 66 percent means that you can increase or decrease the sharpening effect by adjusting the layer opacity up or down.

Figure 5-35 shows the effects of adjusting the layer opacity.

Figure 5-35
Sharpening layer opacity

Layer opacity at 66 percent

Layer opacity at 30 percent

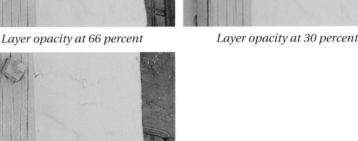

Layer opacity at 100 percent

Finer control is offered by editing the layer mask. You can use any of Photoshop's tools to edit the layer mask, but the one I use most often is Levels.

Levels and the layer mask. Photoshop's Levels command offers an easy yet powerful way to edit the layer mask. Remember the basic rule of masks—white reveals, black conceals—so you can influence the sharpening in several ways by editing the sharpening layer mask. Figure 5-36 shows how each control in Levels affects the sharpening layer.

I rely heavily on presets for my sharpening because I process lots of images, and I find that the combination of the layer opacity and mask editing lets me tweak the sharpening to produce results that very similar to those I would have achieved doing the entire process by hand.

Figure 5-36
Levels and masks

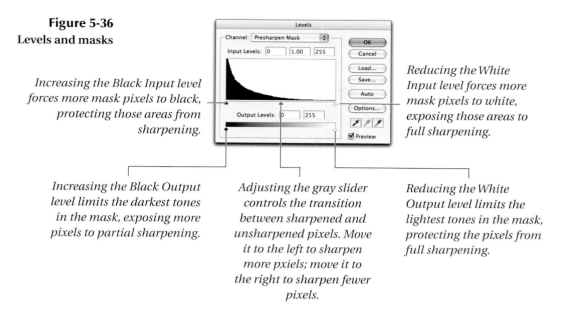

Increasing the Black Input level forces more mask pixels to black, protecting those areas from sharpening.

Reducing the White Input level forces more mask pixels to white, exposing those areas to full sharpening.

Increasing the Black Output level limits the darkest tones in the mask, exposing more pixels to partial sharpening.

Adjusting the gray slider controls the transition between sharpened and unsharpened pixels. Move it to the left to sharpen more pxiels; move it to the right to sharpen fewer pixels.

Reducing the White Output level limits the lightest tones in the mask, protecting the pixels from full sharpening.

Figure 5-37 shows a typical layer mask edit with Levels.

Figure 5-37
Editing the mask
with Levels

The entire image

This Levels edit forces more sharpening into the shadow above the arch, while protecting the sky.

Simple Levels edits like the one shown in Figure 5-37 take care of the vast majority of fine-tuning requirements. In more extreme situations I may resort to Curves, for fine-tuning very specific tonal ranges of the mask.

If the mask starts to exhibit objectionable posterization (meaning that you see sharp transitions between sharpened and unsharpened pixels), Gaussian Blur can help by making more tones available. Gaussian Blur will also soften the mask, of course, but you can use the gray slider in Levels, or a Curves adjustment, to "choke" the softened edges back, if indeed that's what you want to do. Very subtle adjustments can be achieved this way.

Figure 5-37
Editing the mask
with Levels, *continued*

*Image detail at 300%
zoom before editing
the mask*

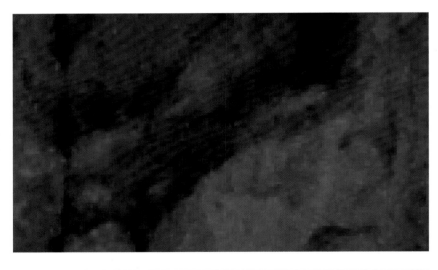

The unedited mask

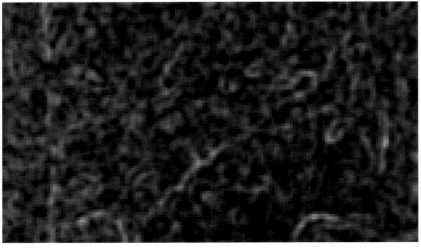

Automating Content Sharpening

You can take the action described earlier for source sharpening and turn it into a complete presharpening routine. You'll need to make at least two separate actions, one for source sharpening that uses a blurred layer to make the mask, the other for source sharpening that calculates the mask layer directly from the presharpening layer. If you want to incorporate noise reduction too, you'll need to create separate actions with and without noise reduction.

Figure 5-37
Editing the mask
with Levels, *continued*

*Image detail at 300%
zoom after editing
the mask*

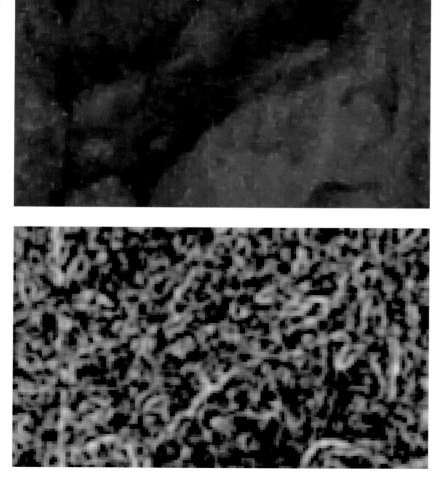

The edited mask

Then you'll have to decide whether you want to create multiple actions with presets for different image sources and resolutions, or toggle the dialog boxes on for those steps where the numbers depend on the image.

A complete presharpening action. Here is a procedure for creating an action that applies sharpening for both source and content in a single routine. In this example, I'll use the values that are appropriate for a mid-frequency 8-megapixel capture, but I'll also point out the steps where you'd vary the numbers for other image types.

I start with the action previously described for automating source optimization. To extend it, select the last action step—Unsharp Mask—and click the Record button in the Actions palette. It's a good idea to open a suitable image and run the source optimization action on it before starting to extend the action—see Figure 5-38.

Figure 5-38
Extending the source optimization action

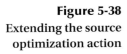

Run the source optimization action.

Once it has completed, select the last step and click Record.

Press Command-Option-Shift-E (Option-Merge Visible) to create a new layer containing a merged copy of the image.

Run Gaussian Blur with Radius 2 pixels.

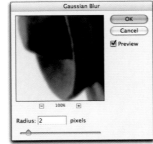

Figure 5-38
Extending the source
optimization action,
continued

*Create a new channel
using Calculations.*

*Name the channel, then
run the Find Edges filter.*

*Run Levels, then press
Command-I to invert
the channel.*

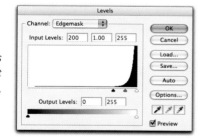

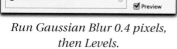

*Run Gaussian Blur 0.4 pixels,
then Levels.*

Figure 5-38
Extending the source
optimization action,
continued

*Load the channel as
a selection, target the
Presharpening layer, and
click the Add layer mask
button in the Layers
palette.*

*For good housekeeping,
delete the Edgemask
channel and the blurred
layer, then run Unsharp
Mask with Amount 200,
Radius 0.8, Threshold
0, and click the Stop
button in the Actions
palette.*

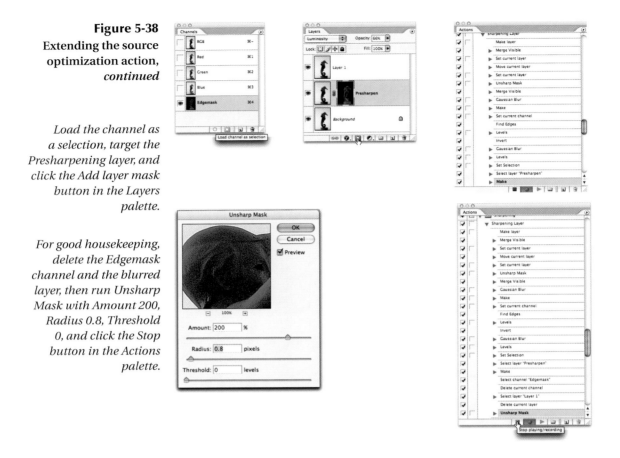

To exercise manual control while you're running the action, turn on the
dialog boxes for the steps shown in Figure 5-39.

Figure 5-39
Actions with
manual control

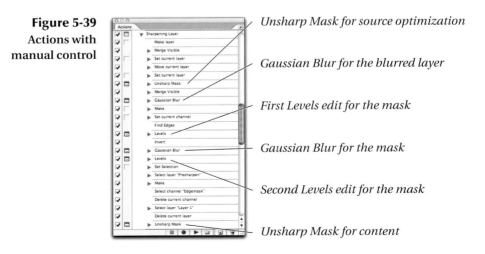

Unsharp Mask for source optimization

Gaussian Blur for the blurred layer

First Levels edit for the mask

Gaussian Blur for the mask

Second Levels edit for the mask

Unsharp Mask for content

Controlling File Size

Sharpening and noise reduction layers and masks add significantly to the size of the file. A single sharpening layer doubles the size of the file, and each extra channel or layer mask adds one-third of the original file size. So file sizes can balloon quite quickly.

Of course, the only way to retain complete control over the sharpening is to keep the layers intact, and take the hit on file size. Other sensible strategies are:

► Once you've tweaked the sharpening to your satisfaction, archive the layered file and continue to work on a flattened copy.

► Once you've tweaked the sharpening to your satisfaction, simply flatten the image.

► To retain some degree of control over the sharpening, create a new layer using Option-Merge Visible, then delete the sharpening layers and masks. Note that the merged layer will be a Normal blend layer with 100 percent opacity, so you won't be able to reduce the sharpening. You can work around this by increasing the opacity of the sharpening layer to 100 percent before creating the merged layer, then you can reduce the opacity of the merged layer to the strength you preferred.

Creative Sharpening

Creative sharpening is the catch-all term for localized adjustments to detail. I include blurring as well as sharpening—one way to make a subject appear sharper is to blur its surroundings a little. Unlike the optimizations for source, content, and output processes, creative adjustments can't be applied automatically—they require creative judgment, hence the name.

But automation plays an important role in making many of the tools I use to do creative sharpening. The only part of the process that can't be automated is the actual localizing of the effect to a specific area of the image. So in this section I'll discuss building creative sharpening (and blurring) tools, and applying them effectively to images. The first valuable lesson to learn is that you can turn any adjustment into a brush!

Effects Brushes

You can turn any adjustment into a brush using three simple steps:

▶ Make the adjustment on a separate layer—usually you'll create the layer using Option-Merge Visible, then apply the adjustment globally to the entire layer.

▶ Add a layer mask set to Hide All—that is, solid black. The easiest way to do so is to Option-click the Add layer mask button in the Layers palette. This hides the effect.

▶ Select the brush tool with the desired size, hardness, and opacity, and paint with white on the layer mask to reveal the effect.

This deceptively simple technique offers very precise control over localized sharpening. Figure 5-40 shows the steps for creating a simple sharpening brush.

Figure 5-40
Creating a simple
sharpening brush

*Create a new layer using
Option-Merge Visible.*

*Run an effect that's stronger
than the desired result.*

*Option-click the Add layer mask
button to add a layer mask that hides
the effect. Now you're ready to brush.*

Tip: Option-Merge Visible. Option-Merge Visible (which when recorded appears in the Actions palette as Stamp Visible) is an invaluable tool for creating layers with merged copies of the image as a basis for sharpening.

In Photoshop CS2, it behaves a little differently from previous versions in that it isn't always necessary to create a new layer before choosing Option-Merge Visible, or pressing Command-Shift-Option-E. If the image already contains at least two layers, Photoshop will add a new one automatically. However, if the image only contains one layer, Option-Merge Visible does nothing. So if you record Option-Merge Visible in actions, *always* record an explicit step that adds a layer before recording the Option-Merge Visible step—that way, the action will work on flat files as well as layered ones.

For a more nuanced sharpening brush, use the Layer Style dialog box to set the blend mode to Luminosity and the layer opacity to 66 percent, then use the Blend If sliders to protect the extreme highlights and shadows. See Figure 5-41.

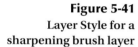

Figure 5-41
Layer Style for a
sharpening brush layer

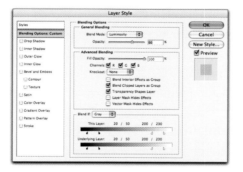

The Luminosity blend mode prevents color shifts, the 66 percent opacity allows you to adjust the strength of the effect up or down, and the Blend If sliders make sure that you leave headroom for the output sharpening.

Working with brushes. When I paint in sharpening or smoothing effects, I always use soft (0% hardness) brushes at low opacities. The softness prevents sharp unnatural-looking transitions between the affected and unaffected areas, and the low opacity helps me "sneak up" on the desired sharpness.

Sometimes, though, I'll go too far and paint in more sharpness or smoothing than I wanted. I can press Undo, or go back a few History states, but it's often easier to switch the foreground and background colors by pressing the X key with no modifiers, then paint the offending adjustment out by painting black on the layer mask.

Tip: Use before-and-after viewing. When you're aiming for subtle sharpening effects, it isn't always easy to see the result of your paint strokes because the adjustment is being made gradually. Turning the layer on and off by clicking the eyeball icon in the Layers palette provides a before-and-after view that makes the effect much more obvious.

A sharpening brush in action. Figure 5-42 shows a sharpening brush created using the steps in Figure 5-40, modified by the Layer Style options in Figure 5-41, applied to an image. Adding extra sharpness to eyes is probably the single most common creative sharpening task.

The brush layer had very strong sharpening applied—Unsharp Mask at Amount 500, Radius 1.2, Threshold 0—but the combination of a 66 percent layer opacity and a 20 percent brush opacity let me achieve a subtle sharpening effect with a few brush strokes.

Notice that the layer mask doesn't contain any pure white. The full-strength effect, even with the reduced layer opacity, would be quite grotesque! Applying a much stronger effect than the desired final result, then brushing it in gradually, offers very fine control over the effect:

Sharpening brush strategies. You don't have to do everything with the brush, though it's often easiest to do so. The goal of the brushing is to localize the effect, and to obtain the desired relative strength of the effect within the brushed area. But in addition to black and white brush strokes, you have two other important controls over the effect:

▶ You can increase or reduce the layer opacity as a master control over the strength of the effect.

▶ You can make tonal edits to the layer mask using Levels or Curves to adjust the way the effect is applied locally.

Sharpening brush actions. The grunt work of setting up a sharpening brush is repetitive, and hence is an obvious candidate for actions. You can build a library of sharpening brushes with different Unsharp Mask settings, or you can build a single action and turn on the dialog box for the Unsharp Mask step. Figure 5-43 shows the steps required to create the sharpening brush I used in Figure 5-42.

Figure 5-42
A sharpening
brush applied

*Image detail optimized
for source and content,
before the sharpening
brush*

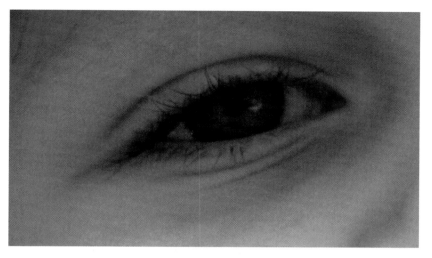

*Image detail optimized
for source and content,
after the sharpening
brush*

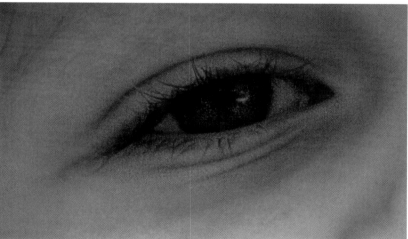

The brush layer mask

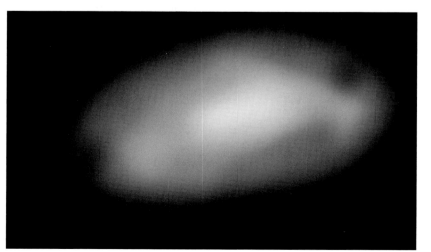

Figure 5-43
Making a sharpening
brush action

*Create a new action, and
start recording. Then
create a new layer, and
choose Option-Merge
Visible.*

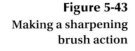
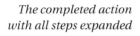

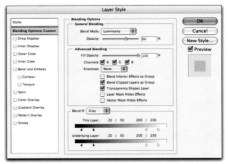

Set the Layer Style options.

*Run the Unsharp
Mask filter.*

*Option-click the Add layer mask button
to add a solid black layer mask, then
select the Brush tool, and click the Stop
button in the Actions palette to stop
recording.*

*The completed action
with all steps expanded*

To use the same action for different sharpening brushes, just turn on the dialog box for the Unsharp Mask step. Or you can duplicate the action and rerecord the Unsharp Mask step (Option-double-click the step) to build a library of sharpening brushes.

Special Sharpening Brushes

Sharpening brushes are useful for more than just applying a little extra local sharpness. You can create all sorts of special-purpose brushes that address specific problems. The only limit is your own ingenuity.

Here are three examples of special sharpening brushes that I find particularly useful.

Depth-of-field-brush. You can't really counteract insufficient depth of field any more than you can make out-of-focus elements in focus. But you can produce a reasonable illusion of doing so using the following technique, which combines Unsharp Mask and Overlay/High Pass sharpening.

Make a sharpening layer using the steps shown in Figure 5-43, but use the Layer Style options shown in Figure 5-44.

Figure 5-44
Layer Styles for
depth of field brush

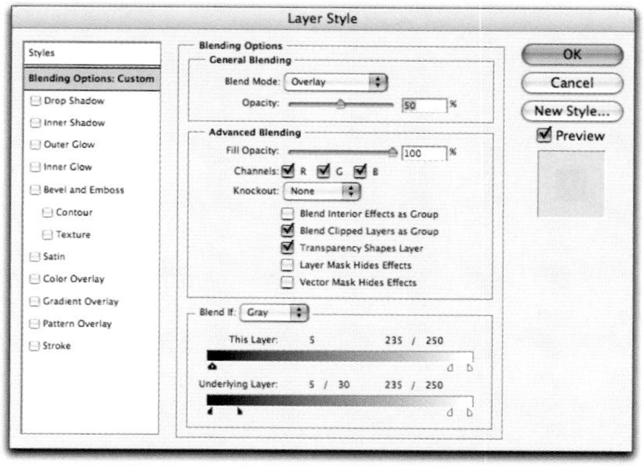

The differences are that the blend mode is set to Overlay, the layer opacity is set to 50 percent, and the Blend If sliders are set to give less protection to the extreme shadows and highlights.

Then, instead of the Unsharp Mask step, run Unsharp Mask with Amount 500 percent, Radius 4 pixels, and Threshold 0, and follow it immediately with High Pass, Radius 25 pixels. Then you can continue to add the layer mask and select the brush.

The effect is something between conventional sharpening and a midtone contrast boost. It's often quite difficult to see the effect while you're painting it in, but turning the layer on and off makes it quite obvious. Figure 5-45 shows its effect on an image.

Figure 5-45 A depth-of-field brush

Before applying the depth-of-field brush   *After applying the depth-of-field brush*

I applied the depth-of-field brush to both the distant elements and to the soft elements in the immediate foreground, producing a fairly convincing illusion of increased depth of field.

A haze-cutting brush. The haze-cutting brush is a variant of the depth-of-field brush that's useful for bringing distant elements in landscapes closer. It uses the same techniques as the depth-of-field brush, but incorporates a warming step immediately after creating the sharpening layer.

Create the sharpening layer as in the previous examples, then add a Solid Color Fill layer with a warming filter color (the exact color specifications depend on your working space of choice—for ProPhoto RGB I use RGB 255, 173, 45), and set the blend mode to Color and the layer opacity to 6 percent. Then choose Merge Down from the Layer menu or press Command-E—see Figure 5-46.

Figure 5-46
Adding a warming
step to cut haze

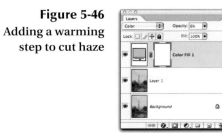

Add a Solid Color layer with a warming color, set to Color blend mode and 6 percent opacity.

Then choose Merge Down from the Layer menu or press Command-E.

The rest of the technique is identical to that for the depth-of-field brush. Figure 5-47 shows it applied to an image.

Figure 5-47   A haze-cutting brush

Before applying the haze-cutting brush   *After applying the haze-cutting brush*

I applied the haze-cutting brush to the hills in the background. It's often quite hard to see the effect as you're applying it, but turning the layer on and off to see before-and-after views makes it quite obvious.

A texture brush. Be warned that this is an extreme effect that should be used with caution! Instead of applying a single Unsharp Mask step, it applies Unsharp Mask multiple times with different Radius settings, using the Fade command between each application. It can do a creditable job of creating realistic texture from minute variations in pixel values.

To create this kind of brush, use the same technique as for a smple sharpening brush, but instead of the single Unsharp Mask step, do the following:

▶ Run Unsharp Mask with Amount 100, Radius 0.5, Threshold 6, then choose Edit>Fade, and choose 50% opacity, Luminosity blend mode.

▶ Run Unsharp Mask with Amount 500, Radius 0.5, Threshold 3, then choose Edit>Fade, and choose 25% opacity, Luminosity blend mode.

▶ Run Unsharp Mask with Amount 500, Radius 1, Threshold 3, then choose Edit>Fade, and choose 25% opacity, Luminosity blend mode.

▶ Run Unsharp Mask with Amount 300, Radius 4, Threshold 3, then choose Edit>Fade, and choose 25% opacity, Luminosity blend mode.

▶ Run Unsharp Mask with Amount 100, Radius 8, Threshold 0, then choose Edit>Fade, and choose 25% opacity, Luminosity blend mode.

▶ Run Unsharp Mask with Amount 100, Radius 16, Threshold 0, then choose Edit>Fade, and choose 25% opacity, Luminosity blend mode.

Then apply the layer mask and select the brush tool. You may want to set the default layer opacity to 50 percent rather than 66 percent, because this really is a pretty strong effect. Credit for this one goes to my friend and colleague Jeff Schewe.

Figure 5-48 shows the texture brush effect applied to an image. I applied the brush to the painted walls at an opacity of 40 percent, and to the wooden doors at an opacity of 20 percent. I left the foreground untouched.

These examples should give you some hint of just how much you can do with sharpening brushes. I will, however, caution you to save their use for the images that really deserve them!

Figure 5-48   A texture brush

Before applying the texture brush   *After applying the texture brush*

Smoothing Brushes

Smoothing brushes are the other side of the coin from sharpening brushes, and use the same basic techniques. You can make simple smoothing brushes by substituting a low-radius Gaussian Blur for the Unsharp Mask step in the simple sharpening brush.

But Gaussian Blur can very quickly lead to an unnatural appearance that proclaims digital manipulation. You can achieve a more convincing result if you add a little noise immediately after applying Gaussian Blur to the brush layer. I use the Add Noise filter set to add 2–5% Gaussian noise with monochromatic unchecked to break up the plasticky-looking digital perfection produced by Gaussian Blur.

Figure 5-49 shows a smoothing brush applied to an image (it shows what I would have looked like when I was 25 if I'd known then what I know now! (And yes, I had the hair loss when I was 25.)

Figure 5-49
A smoothing brush
with noise

Before the
smoothing brush

After the
smoothing brush

Smoothing brushes such as this one are great for fixing skin blemishes and for smoothing out unwanted texture, but if you need, for example, to knock back a distracting background or to smooth out noise in a sky, you really need a smoothing brush that protects the edges in the image. Otherwise you have to take extreme pains to avoid wiping out important detail, such as where the sky meets the skyline.

An edge-protected smoothing brush. I've already shown you how to make an edge mask. But a layer can only have one layer mask, so to combine an edge mask with a brush layer requires a little ingenuity. Here's how I do it.

I start by using Option-Merge Visible to create a brush layer, then I use the techniques I described earlier in the chapter to create an edge mask. I load it as a selection, then apply the selection to the brush layer as a layer mask. Next, I choose Layer>Layer Mask>Apply, which applies the layer mask to the layer, then deletes it. The result is a layer that has transparency where the edges would be. Now I can add a brush mask, and brush the blurring in without worrying about getting too close to the edges.

Figure 5-50 shows an image before and after the application of an edge-protected smoothing brush.

Figure 5-50   **An edge-protected smoothing brush**

Before applying the smoothing brush   *After applying the smoothing brush*

The edge-protected smoothing brush allows me to knock back the distracting textures in the background so that the subjects pops, without having to be particularly careful around the edges.

Creative Sharpening Rules

Very few rules apply to creative sharpening, which in part is why I call it creative sharpening! The big ones are:

▶ Always perform creative sharpening or smoothing at the image's native resolution. Remember, the goal is to create a use-neutral master image that you can repurpose through different kinds of output sharpening at different sizes.

▶ Don't overdo things. While judging final sharpness from the computer display is quite unreliable, if things look overdone at the creative phase, it's likely that they'll look that way in the final output too.

Ultimately, control of detail is just as important a creative function as control of tone or color, even if it tends to get much less attention. So absorb these techniques and let your creativity flow!

Sharpening for Output

Where optimizing for content and creative sharpening require human skill, sharpening for output is essentially a deterministic process, since any given print process always turns pixels into marks on paper the same way no matter the input. Creativity at this stage is not only unneccesary, but should be actively discouraged.

In the previous workflow phases, we tried to avoid obvious sharpening haloes. When we sharpen for print, haloes are not only desirable, but necessary. The trick is to keep them small enough that they don't appear as discrete features on the print when viewed at reasonable viewing distances.

The rule of thumb that has served me well is to keep the sharpening haloes no smaller than 1/100th of an inch and no larger than 1/50th of an inch, with the smaller number being preferred for small (up to 11 x 14-inch) prints, dropping to the larger number as dictated by the resolution of the image and the size of the print.

Some pundits recommend resampling images to reach print resolution. I cheerfully downsample images, particularly for halftone printing where it's certain that any additional resolution beyond 2.5 times the screen frequency will simply be discarded. But I tend to avoid upsampling unless there's really no choice. I've made a good many satisfying 20-inch prints from an 8-megapixel camera by sending the printer 180 real pixels per inch. I've yet to see a benefit to forcing Photoshop to make up more pixels by upsampling.

If you're trying to make much larger prints from an 8-megapixel camera, you'll have to upsample, but be warned that the results tend to be reminiscent of making huge prints from 35mm film.

Do the Math

With the goal of the sharpening haloes in mind, remember that all you can do is to sharpen the pixels themselves. So the amount of sharpening required is a function of the size of the pixels, which in turn is a function of the resolution you're sending to the output process.

For example, this book is printed using a 150-line-per-inch screen, and most of the images are printed at 300 pixels per inch. Simple arithmetic dictates that a halo of 1/100th of an inch is 3 pixels wide, so that's my goal when I sharpen images for this print process.

For larger prints at lower resolutions, the same-sized halo will obviously have smaller pixel dimensions. At 180 ppi, which I regard as the lower limit for inkjet printing, a 1/100th-inch halo is 1.8 pixels wide, and a 1/50th-inch halo is 3.6 pixels wide, so again a 3-pixel halo is a reasonable aim point.

Output Sharpening Techniques

The first and most important rule in output sharpening is that it *must* be done at the final output resolution, after any required resampling. There are no exceptions to this rule.

For halftone sharpening, I use plain old Unsharp Mask on a layer set to Luminosity blending at 66 percent opacity. In practice, it's extremely rare that I'll adjust the layer opacity of the output sharpening layer, but it's always nice to know that I can!

I also set the Blend If sliders to the values shown in Figure 5-51. There's really no point in applying sharpening to pixels lighter than level 250 (which in halftone terms is a 1 percent dot), and I feather off the sharpening in the deep shadows below level 10 (which is a 99 percent dot).

Figure 5-51
Halftone sharpening
at 300 ppi

*I create an Option-
Merge Visible layer with
the Layer Style options
at near right, then I
apply Unsharp Mask
with the settings at
far right.*

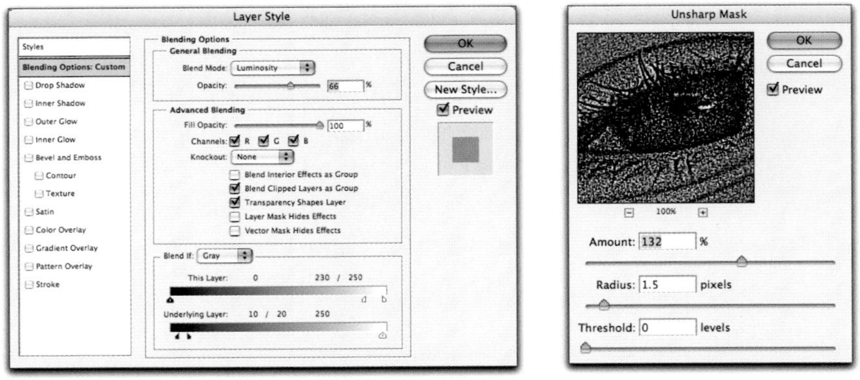

Halftone sharpening. The very simple sharpening shown in Figure 5-50 works very well for 300 ppi, 150 lpi halftone printing on coated paper. For uncoated papers, I increase the Amount setting in Unsharp Mask to 158. I arrived at these numbers empirically, which is to say, by trial and error, but they have now been through extensive testing on tens of thousands of images, and I stand by them.

Figure 5-52 shows an image before and after output sharpening for this book's halftone process. For lower screen freqencies, I use a smaller Radius value and a higher Amount, and for higher screen frequencies I use a larger Radius and a lower Amount, always with the goal of keeping the sharpening haloes around 1/100th of an inch.

Inkjet sharpening. Inkjet printers use error-diffusion screening rather than halftone dots, which produces a rather different effect that in turn requires a rather different type of sharpening. I use the same Blend If settings in the Layer Style dialog box as for halftone sharpening, but I use a combination of Unsharp Mask and Overlay/High Pass sharpening.

For a 300 ppi inkjet print on glossy or semi-gloss paper, I create the sharpening layer, but leave it with Normal blending for the Unsharp Mask step, which is Unsharp Mask with Amount 320, Radius 0.6, Threshold 4. I then immediately choose Edit>Fade with Opacity at 70 percent and blend set to Luminosity. Then I set the layer to Overlay blending with an opacity of 50 percent, and run the High Pass filter with a Radius setting of 2 pixels.

Figure 5-52 Before and after output sharpening

Before output sharpening   *After output sharpening*

These actual pixels from the edge of the brim of the hat
show a 3-pixel light contour and a 3-pixel dark contour.

Obviously I can't show you inkjet screening in this book. The results of the inkjet sharpening are very similar in pixel terms to those of the halftone output sharpening, but the haloes are very slightly more intense for the inkjet sharpening than they are for the halftone sharpening even though they're the same size. The tighter dither of the inkjet screen can render the contrast a little more precisely than halftone output can, so the higher contrast is effective. Figure 5-53 shows a detail from the image in Figure 5-52, comparing halftone sharpening and inkjet sharpening.

*Halftone sharpening
at 300% view*

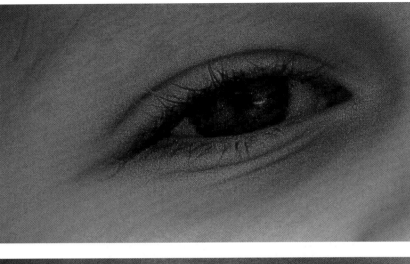

*Inkjet sharpening
at 300% view*

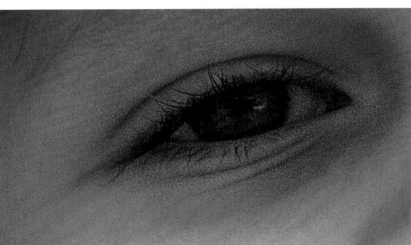

Continuous-tone sharpening. For continuous-tone printers such as the Durst Lambda or the Fuji Frontier, I use the same sharpening technique as for inkjet, but with slightly different values (which again were the product of much trial-and-error testing). For 300 ppi output, I use Unsharp Mask with Amount 350, Radius 0.6, Threshold 4, faded to 70 percent opacity with Luminosity blend mode, then I set the layer to Overlay at 50 percent opacity and run the High Pass filter with a Radius of 1.5 pixels.

For lower resolutions, I use smaller Radius settings and higher Amount settings, and for higher resolutions I use larger Radius settings and lower Amount settings, always keeping in mind the final size of the sharpening haloes.

Magic Numbers

The numbers I've quoted for the sharpening settings for different output processes may seem like voodoo, but they're the product of exhaustive testing, and I use them every day. That said, it's entirely possible that you can come up with numbers that you prefer to mine.

If you wish to do so, take heed of this key piece of advice: The only way to evaluate print sharpening is to sharpen the image, make a print, and examine it carefully. Looking at image pixels on the screen can give you a gross picture of the size of the sharpening haloes, but subtle differences like the ones shown in Figure 5-53 can only be evaluated in the print itself.

The Power of the Workflow

The biggest advantage of the sharpening workflow I've described in this chapter is that images receive optimal sharpening. That in itself is no small thing. But an equally significant advantage is that images receive optimal *use-neutral* sharpening, so you can easily repurpose them for different outputs and sizes.

Decoupling the image source and image content concerns from the demands of the output process makes sense from both a quality and a productivity standpoint. It's conceivable that at some point in the future, savvy printer vendors will build optimal output sharpening into RIPs and printer drivers so that we can deliver images without having to worry about output size and resolution.

Looking even further forward, it's at least conceptually possible that display profiles could contain sharpness parameters that controlled anti-aliasing to the display, ironing out differences in sharpness the way they do color differences today. But in the here and now, it's fair to say that control of detail is a subject that has received far less attention than control of tone and color. This book is a small step toward redressing the balance, but a great deal of work remains to be done.

In the next, final chapter, I'll demonstrate case studies that show the entire sharpening workflow applied to images of different types from different sources.

6

Case
Studies

Sharpening from Capture to Print

In this final chapter, I put into practice what I've been preaching for the past 200-odd pages. I've selected images from very different sources, at many different quality levels, because every image can be improved by good control of detail.

Each image is fed through the same workflow:

▶ Optimization for image source

▶ Optimization for image content

▶ Creative sharpening or smoothing

▶ Optimization for output

The first step is to evaluate the image and decide how to handle it. Does the image need noise reduction? What is the dominant feature I wish to emphasize in optimizing for content? Once these questions have been answered and the optimization carried out, does the image need any localized adjustments? After carrying out any localized work, the image is saved as a use-neutral master ready for repurposing for different outputs.

I can only show one output process, the one used for this book, but for each image I've included final sharpened output at a variety of different sizes to show the flexibility of the sharpening workflow.

Large-Format Transparency

This image was scanned from a 4 by 5 transparency at 1600 ppi, creating a file with pixel dimensions of 6950 x 8572. At 300 ppi, the full image would measure approximately 23 by 28.5 inches. Figure 6-1 shows a detail at 300 ppi, and a zoomed-in view that approximates 400 percent zoom on screen. The full image is shown in Figure 6-2.

Looking at the zoomed-in view, I see some color noise that could cause problems with sharpening, so the first task is to reduce the color noise. With relatively mild color noise like this, it's tempting to overlook it and just start sharpening the image—at small reproduction sizes, the noise will largely be resampled out of existence. But the goal here is to produce a master file that can be printed at a wide range of sizes, so I deem the color noise reduction a wise investment of a couple of minutes.

Since this is a flat file, I can simply duplicate the Background layer to provide a noise reduction layer. With a layered file, I'd use Option-Merge Visible.

Figure 6-1   A large-format transparency scan, details

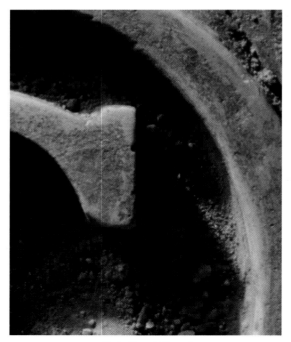

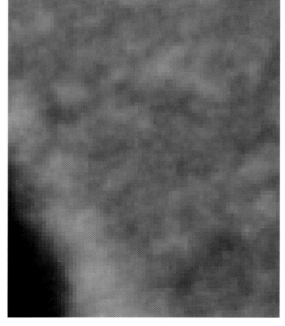

Detail at 300 ppi   *Zoomed in at 400 percent*

Figure 6-2   A large-format transparency scan

A light application of the Reduce Noise filter as shown in Figure 6-3 eliminates the color noise without adding too much softness and, more importantly, without adding artifacts that would be made more obvious by subsequent sharpening, which is the next step—see Figure 6-4.

Figure 6-3   After noise reduction with Reduce Noise

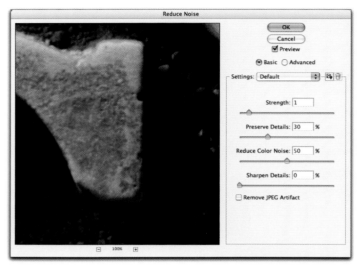

I create a duplicate layer, then I run Reduce Noise with the settings shown at right. I record the settings in the layer name, because otherwise I won't know how the noise reduction was performed.

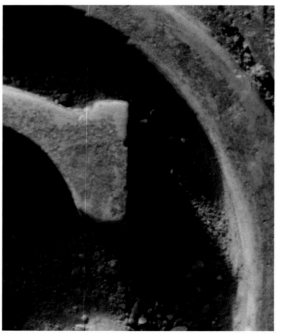

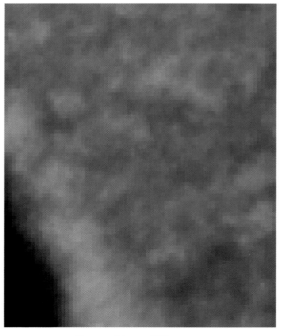

Detail at 300 ppi   *Zoomed in at 400 percent*

Figure 6-4 Applying sharpening for source

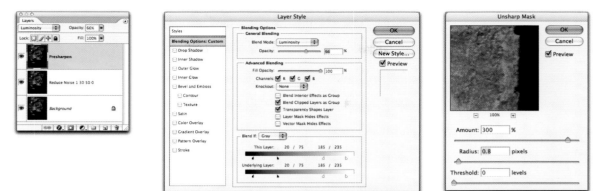

I use Option-Merge Visible to create a sharpening layer, which I set to Luminosity blend mode with 66 percent opacity. Then I set the Blend If sliders to constrain the sharpening to the midtones.

I run the Unsharp Mask filter with Amount 300, Radius 0.8, Threshold 0, to produce the result shown below.

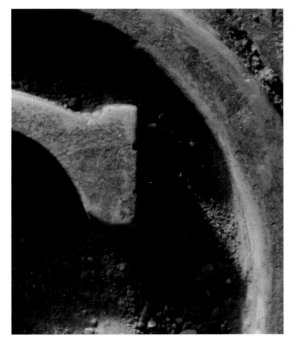

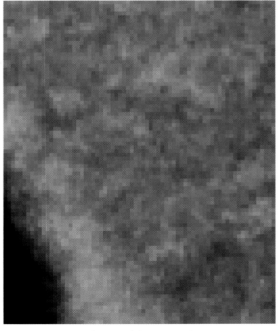

Detail at 300 ppi

Zoomed in at 400%

To sharpen for content, I make an edge mask which I apply to the sharpening layer as a layer mask. Then I apply Unsharp Mask to the masked layer—see Figure 6-5.

Figure 6-5   Applying sharpening for content

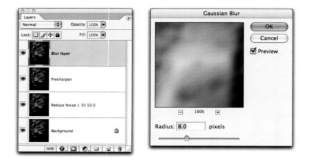

I use Option-Merge Visible to create a blur layer, then I run Gaussian Blur on the blur layer with a Radius of 8 pixels.

I use Calculations to create a blur channel from the blur layer, below left, then I run the Find Edges filter on the channel, below right.

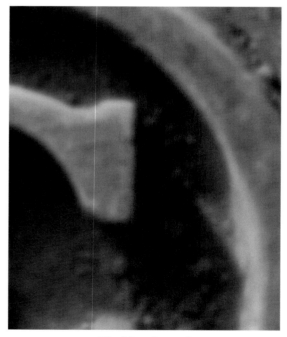

The blur channel

The blur channel after Find Edges

I adjust the mask channel with Levels, then I Invert it to create white edges rather than black ones. I run Gaussian Blur again, and follow it with a second levels tweak to produce the final mask channel.

Figure 6-5 Applying sharpening for content, *continued*

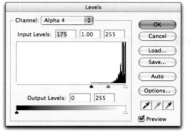

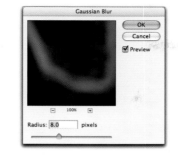

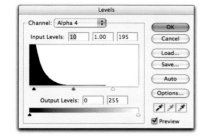

Levels before Invert

Levels after Invert

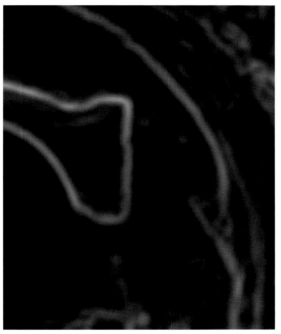

The final edge mask

*I load the mask channel as a selection, then
I load the selection as a layer mask for the
sharpening layer. Once the mask is loaded, I
delete both the blur layer and the edge mask
channel, because they've served their purpose
and are no longer needed.*

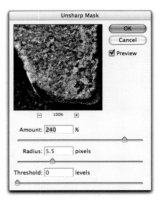

*I target the sharpening layer (the previous step left
the mask, rather than the layer, targeted), and run
Unsharp Mask with Amount 240 and Radius 5.5.
The preview in Unsharp Mask's proxy window is
quite misleading because it doesn't show the
constraining effects of the layer mask and
the Layer Style settings.*

Figure 6-5 Applying sharpening for content, *continued*

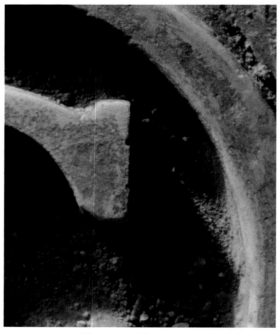

Sharpened for content

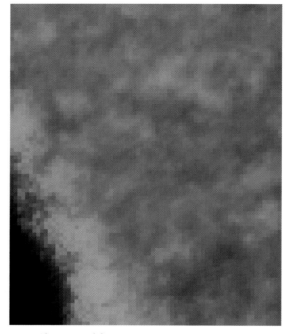

Sharpened for content, 400 percent zoom

At 400 percent zoom, the wide edges look alarmingly crunchy. Remember, though, that on final output, the pixels that look scary will be very small indeed. Examining image pixels at high magnification (which some refer to in a derogatory fashion as "pixel-peeping") is a good way to learn what happens when you sharpen images, but tells you very little about final image appearance. For halftone output, 25 percent view is probably the least inaccurate on-screen view.

The noise reduction, source sharpening, and content sharpening create a use-neutral version of the image that I can repurpose for different output sizes and resolutions. I always archive the layered files, but at this stage in the workflow I flatten a copy of the image and use the flattened copy for any further work.

Output sharpening must always be done at the final print resolution, so if any resampling is required, it must be done before applying the output sharpening. For downsampling, I always use Photoshop's Bicubic Sharper option to downsample, while on the rare occasions that I upsample, I use Bicubic Smoother.

The output sharpening for this book, applied to 300-ppi images, is quite simple. I create a layer using Option-Merge Visible, and set it to Luminosity blend mode at 66 percent opacity, using the Blend If sliders to protect the extreme highlights and shadows. Then I run Unsharp Mask with Amount 132 and Radius 1.5. Figure 6-6 shows the output sharpening settings, the entire image downsampled to 300 ppi, then sharpened for output, and a 300-ppi detail at the image's native resolution, also sharpened for output.

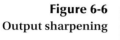

Figure 6-6
Output sharpening

To apply output sharpening, I create a new layer using Option-Merge Visible.

I set the Layer Style options as shown at right. Luminosity blending avoids color shifts, the 66 percent opacity gives me some control after sharpening, and the Blend If sliders protect the extreme highlights and shadows.

I apply the final output sharpening using Unsharp Mask with Amount 132, Radius 1.5 pixels, and Threshold 0.

Figure 6-6   Output sharpening, *continued*

Full image downsampled to 300 ppi, then sharpened for output

Figure 6-6 Output sharpening, *continued*

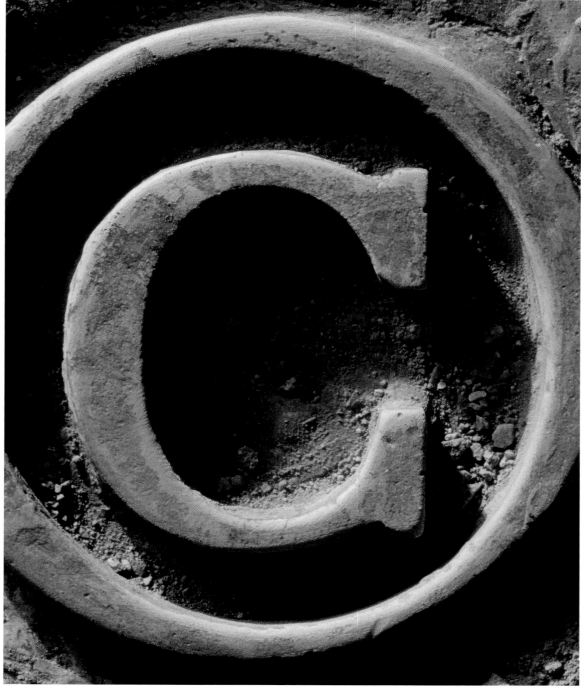

A 300 ppi detail at native resolution, sharpened for output

A 35mm Color Negative

This image was scanned from a 35mm color negative at 5760 ppi, creating a file with pixel dimensions of 5150 by 7400. At 300 ppi, the full image would measure approximately 17 by 24.5 inches, but I wouldn't attempt to print it at that size. I scan 35mm film at the very high resolution of 6300 ppi because I've found that if I do the detail work—noise reduction and sharpening—at 6300 ppi, then downsample to a more reasonable 4000 ppi, I get better results than I would if I started with a 4000-ppi scan.

Figure 6-7 shows a detail at 300 ppi, and a zoomed-in view that approximates 200 percent zoom on screen. The full image is shown in Figure 6-8. Looking at the zoomed-in view, I see heavy color noise that will definitely cause problems with sharpening, so the first task is to reduce the color noise. For heavy noise like this, I rely on the Despeckle filter applied differentially to each channel.

Figure 6-7   A 35mm color negative scan, details

300 ppi detail   *200 percent zoom*

Figure 6-8
A 35mm color
negative scan

Figure 6-8
A 35mm color
negative scan

Since this is a flat file, I can simply duplicate the Background layer to provide a noise reduction layer. With a layered file, I'd use Option-Merge Visible. Figure 6-9 shows the noise reduction process, running the Despeckle filter on a layer set to Normal blending with 100 percent opacity.

Figure 6-9 Noise reduction with Despeckle

The red channel

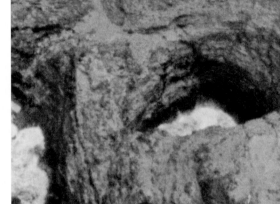

The red channel after Despeckle

The green channel

The red channel after Despeckle twice

Figure 6-9   Noise reduction with Despeckle, *continued*

The blue channel

The blue channel after Despeckle four times

The composite image after Despeckle

After Despeckle, zoom view

Next, I create a sharpening layer to serve for both source and content optimization using Option-Merge Visible. I set the Layer Style Options as shown in Figure 6-10 and run Unsharp Mask with Amount 200, Radius 1.2.

Figure 6-10   Applying sharpening for source

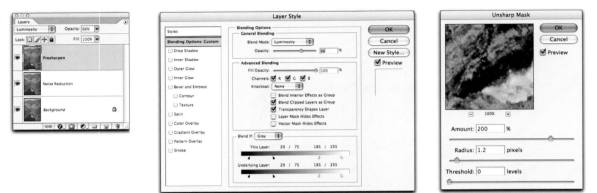

I use Option-Merge Visible to create a sharpening layer, which I set to Luminosity blend mode with 66 percent opacity. Then I set the Blend If sliders to constrain the sharpening to the midtones.

I run the Unsharp Mask filter with Amount 200, Radius 1.2, Threshold 0, to produce the result shown below.

Detail at 300 ppi

Zoomed in at 400 percent

Next, I create an edge mask and sharpen for content. I create a blur layer, extract a blur channel which becomes the basis of the edge mask created with Find Edges, load it as a layer mask on the sharpening layer, and sharpen—see Figure 6-11.

Figure 6-11 Applying sharpening for content

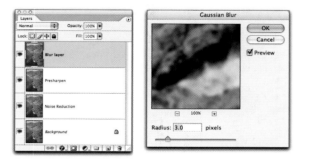

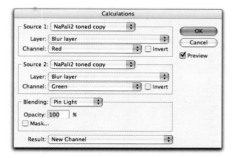

I use Option-Merge Visible to create a blur layer, then I run Gaussian Blur on the blur layer with a Radius of 3 pixels.

I use Calculations to create a blur channel from the blur layer, below left, then I run the Find Edges filter on the channel, below right.

The blur channel

The blur channel after Find Edges

Figure 6-11   Applying sharpening for content, *continued*

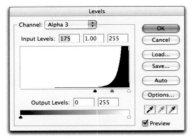

Levels before Invert

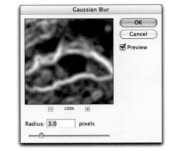

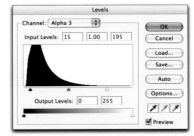

Levels after Invert

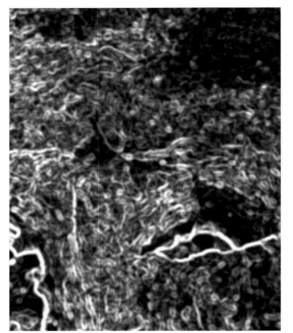

The final edge mask

I load the mask channel as a selection, then I load the selection as a layer mask for the sharpening layer. Once the mask is loaded, I delete both the blur layer and the edge mask channel, because they've served their purpose and are no longer needed.

I target the sharpening layer (the previous step left the mask, rather than the layer, targeted), and run Unsharp Mask with Amount 200 and Radius 0.8. The preview in Unsharp Mask's proxy window is quite misleading because it doesn't show the constraining effects of the layer mask and the Layer Style settings.

Figure 6-11   Applying sharpening for content, *continued*

Sharpened for content   *Sharpened for content, 400 percent zoom*

Before I sharpen for output, I want to do some localized sharpening on the distant hills. I use the haze-cutting brush described in Chapter 5, *Putting the Tools to Work*, to bring the distant hills a little closer—see Figure 6-12.

Figure 6-12   Creative sharpening

Before the haze-cutting brush   *After the haze-cutting brush*

The image is now completely optimized for source and content. I'd deliberately scanned the film at a higher resolution than it could really support so that I could do the detail work at super-high resolution. Now I can downsample the image to a more reasonable 4000 ppi from its original 5760, and archive it as a master file. Figure 6-13 shows image details after downsampling with Bicubic Sharper.

Figure 6-13   Details after downsampling

 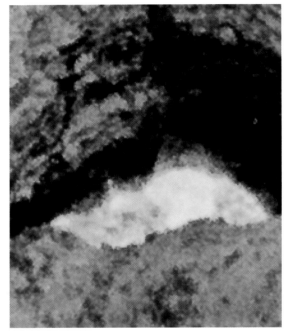

After downsampling   *After downsampling, 400 percent zoom*

Downsampling reduces both the noise and the pixelation along the edges. The resulting image downsampled from 5760 ppi to 4000 ppi is substantially cleaner than anything I could have obtained if I'd scanned at 4000 ppi to begin with. On small-format film, I almost invariably overscan and do the detail work at the scan resolution, then downsample.

Now the image is ready for output sharpening. I use exactly the same formula for output sharpening for all the examples in this chapter, so I won't repeat the steps in detail—they're identical to those in the previous example. Figure 6-14 shows the full image downsampled to fit the page, and a detail at the image's native resolution reproduced at 300 ppi.

Figure 6-14   After output sharpening

Figure 6-14   After output sharpening, *continued*

A Hard-Copy Scan

While I much prefer working from the original film to working from prints (and much prefer working from digital captures to working from film), sometimes the print is all that's available, particularly with old photographs that may have great personal or even historical significance. The image in Figure 6-15 may not have much historical significance, but it does capture perfectly the utter disdain with which I'm treated daily once I've opened the cat food.

Figure 6-15
A hard-copy scan

This image was shot with consumer film in a point-and-shoot camera, and scanned from a 4- by 6-inch drugstore print. I can't really expect to get much enlargement out of it, but I can still improve it. The first task to check the noise to see if it needs special treatment.

Figure 6-16 shows a zoomed-in view of the composite and individual color channels. The blue channel is quite noisy while the others are relatively clean, so I duplicate the Background layer and run the Despeckle filter five times on the blue channel only.

The image is lacking midtone contrast, so the next step is to add a midtone contrast layer. I do so using the techniques described earlier in this book—see "Midtone Contrast" under "Overlay and High Pass" in Chapter 4, *Sharpening Tools and Techniques*.

The midtone contrast layer doesn't really sharpen the image—it applies over a much wider area than the edges in the image—but it has the effect of making the image appear quite a bit sharper. Hence it's important to add midtone contrast before sharpening, otherwise you're likely to over-sharpen. Figure 6-17 shows the image after adding midtone contrast.

Figure 6-16   Checking the channels

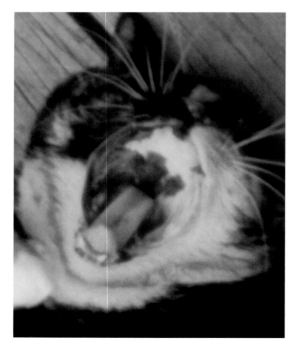 

Composite channel   *Red channel*

Figure 6-16   Checking the channels, *continued*

Green channel

Blue channel

Blue channel after Despeckle 5 times

Composite channel after blue Despeckle

Figure 6-17
After adding
midtone contrast

Next, I create a sharpening layer using Option-Merge Visible. I'll use the sharpening layer to apply sharpening for source, and then, with the addition of a layer mask, for content.

I set the Layer Style options for the sharpening layer to Luminosity blend mode with 66 percent opacity, and use the Blend If sliders to constrain the sharpening to the midtones. Then I run the Unsharp Mask filter with Amount 500, Radius 0.5 pixels, and Threshold 0. Figure 6-18 shows the process of creating the sharpening layer, and the results of applying the sharpening optimization for the image source.

Figure 6-18   Applying sharpening for source

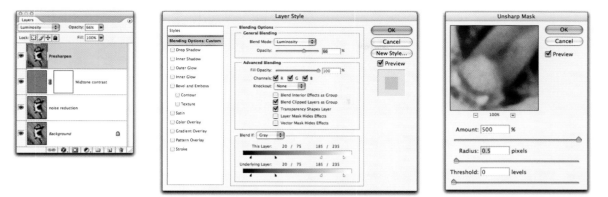

I use Option-Merge Visible to create a sharpening layer, which I set to Luminosity blend mode with 66 percent opacity. Then I set the Blend If sliders to constrain the sharpening to the midtones.

I run the Unsharp Mask filter with Amount 500, Radius 0.5, Threshold 0, to produce the result shown below.

After sharpening for image source

Next, I create an edge mask created from a blur layer, apply it to the sharpening layer as a layer mask, and sharpen for content through the layer mask—see Figure 6-19.

Figure 6-19   Applying sharpening for content

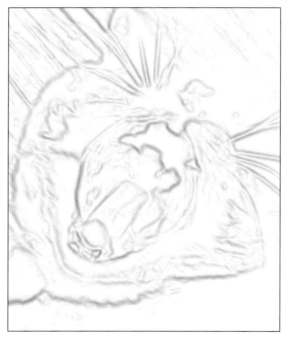

I use Option-Merge Visible to create a blur layer, then I run Gaussian Blur on the blur layer with a Radius of 3 pixels.

I use Calculations to create a blur channel from the blur layer, below left, then I run the Find Edges filter on the channel, below right.

The blur channel

The blur channel after Find Edges

Figure 6-19   Applying sharpening for content, *continued*

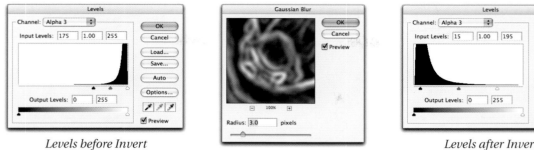

Levels before Invert   *Levels after Invert*

I load the mask channel as a selection, then I load the selection as a layer mask for the sharpening layer, and delete both the blur layer and the edge mask channel.

The final edge mask

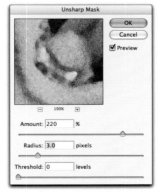

I target the sharpening layer and run Unsharp Mask with Amount 220, Radius 3, and Threshold 0 to produce the result at right.

Sharpened for content

I downsample the image to 300 ppi using Bicubic Sharper, then apply the same output sharpening as in the previous examples to produce the final sharpened image in Figure 6-20.

Figure 6-20
After sharpening
for output

I've been able to make a quite decent 8- by 10-inch inkjet print from this image, which considering its origin as a 4- by 6-inch drugstore print is fairly remarkable. Older prints, especially contact prints, can contain a surprising amount of information, but they won't last forever, especially if they're color prints, so digitize and sharpen them while they're still in reasonable shape.

A Digital JPEG Capture

This image was shot with a 4.2 megapixel Canon Elph set to maximum quality. It produces a file with pixel dimensions of 1704 by 2272 pixels. Figure 6-21 shows the entire image.

Figure 6-21
A JPEG capture

Zooming in, I can see some light JPEG artifacts and some typical JPEG color noise—see Figure 6-22.

Figure 6-22 JPEG artifacts

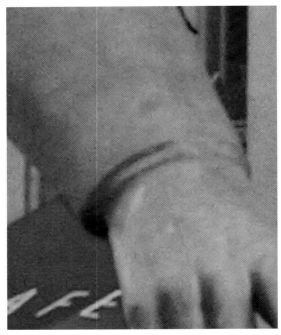 

Detail at 200 percent zoom   *Detail at 200 percent zoom*

Sharpening will make these artifacts worse, so the first task is to reduce the noise. I create a noise reduction layer using Option-Merge Visible (the file already has layers), and run Reduce Noise with the settings shown in Figure 6-23.

Figure 6-23
Noise reduction with
Reduce Noise

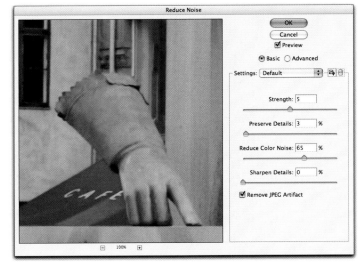

Figure 6-23   Noise reduction with Reduce Noise, *continued*

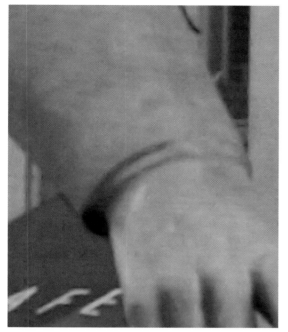

Detail at 200 percent zoom   *Detail at 200 percent zoom*

The settings used here for Reduce Noise are about as strong as I ever use. They seem to do a good job of wiping out the JPEG artifacts, but as you'll see when I start to apply sharpening, they have a tendency to create artifacts of their own. Noise reduction and sharpening have an inherent tendency to fight one another since they basically do opposite things to the image, so I'll have to walk a fine line when I sharpen.

Sharpening for the image source is next. I create a sharpening layer using Option-Merge Visible, set to Luminosty blend at 66 percent opacity, with the Blend If sliders set to constrain the sharpening to the midtones. Then I run the Unsharp Mask filter with Amount 80, Radius 1.0 pixels, and Threshold 0, to produce the results shown in Figure 6-24.

This relatively gentle sharpening is enough to bring back some of the tonal JPEG artifacts (but not the color noise, fortunately). It's futile to try to eliminate these artifacts completely (unless you like images that appear to have been run through a heavy Median filter), so I'll concentrate on keeping them below the threshold of objectionability.

Figure 6-24   Applying sharpening for source

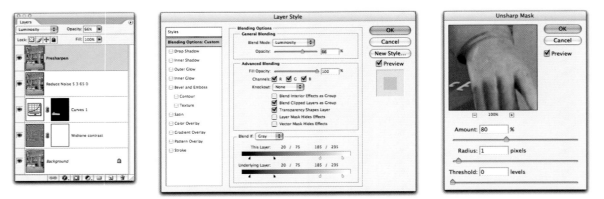

I use Option-Merge Visible to create a sharpening layer, which I set to Luminosity blend mode with 66 percent opacity. Then I set the Blend If sliders to constrain the sharpening to the midtones.

I run the Unsharp Mask filter with Amount 80, Radius 1.0, Threshold 0, to produce the result shown below.

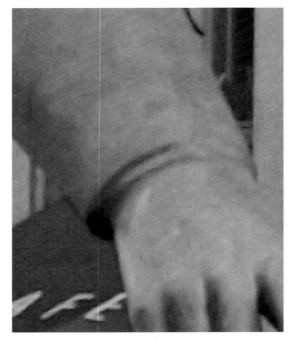

After sharpening for image source

After sharpening for image source

Next, I apply sharpening for content, as shown in Figure 6-25, using the sharpening layer with a mask made from a blur layer.

Figure 6-25   Applying sharpening for content

 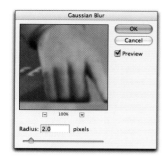

I use Option-Merge Visible to create a blur layer, then I run Gaussian Blur on the blur layer with a Radius of 2 pixels.

I use Calculations to create a blur channel from the blur layer, below left, then I run the Find Edges filter on the channel, below right.

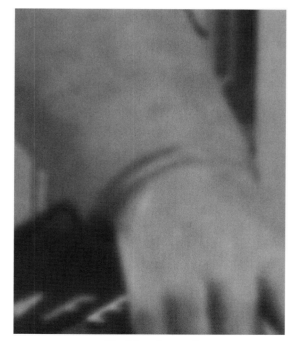

The blur channel

The blur channel after Find Edges

Figure 6-25   Applying sharpening for content, *continued*

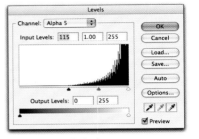

Levels before Invert

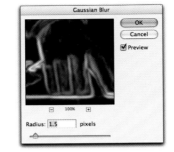

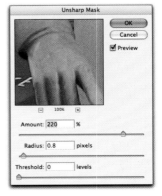

Levels after Invert

I load the mask channel as a selection, then I load the selection as a layer mask for the sharpening layer, and delete both the blur layer and the edge mask channel.

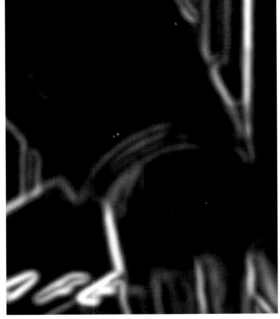

The final edge mask

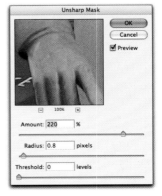

I target the sharpening layer and run Unsharp Mask with Amount 220, Radius 0.8, and Threshold 0 to produce the result at right.

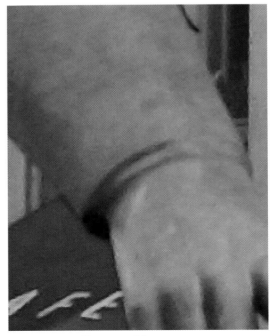

Sharpened for content

This image can be further improved by some selective sharpening and smoothing. I use the edge-protected smoothing brush described in "Smoothing Brushes" in Chapter 5, *Putting the Tools to Work*, to blur the background buildings slightly, producing more of an illusion of depth.

I use a sharpening brush like the one described in "Effects Brushes" in Chapter 5 to add some extra sharpness to the hand and the concrete arch. Finally, I use a depth-of-field brush like the one described in "Special Sharpening Brushes" in Chapter 5 to bring the paving slabs in the foreground into focus. Figure 6-26 shows the image before and after the selective adjustments.

Figure 6-26   **Before and after selective adjustments**

Before selective adjustments   *After selective adjustments*

Finally, I sharpen the image for output using the same sharpening as in all the previous examples. Figure 6-27 shows the full image sharpened for output.

Figure 6-27   Sharpened for output

A Digital Raw Capture

This image was shot as a raw file with a Canon EOS 20D, producing an image with pixel dimensions of 3504 by 2336 pixels. It was converted through Adobe Camera Raw 3.4 to a 16-bit/channel ProPhoto RGB TIFF, with no sharpening, no luminance smoothing, and only a very light color noise reduction of 15.

Although it was shot at ISO 400, it's properly exposed (Camera Raw's Exposure slider was set to 0), and hence has no significant noise problems, even in the shadows, so I won't need to carry out any noise reduction and can focus entirely on sharpening.

Figure 6-28 shows the full image downsampled to 300 ppi to fit the page. Figure 6-29 shows a detail at native resolution, and at a zoomed-in view that approximates 100 percent (Actual Pixels) zoom.

Figure 6-28   A digital raw capture

The full image downsampled to 300 ppi

Figure 6-29 A digital raw capture, details

Native resolution at 300 ppi   *Approximately 100 percent zoom*

First, I apply sharpening for the image source, using the same kind of sharpening layer I've used in the previous examples—see Figure 6-30.

Figure 6-30 Applying sharpening for source

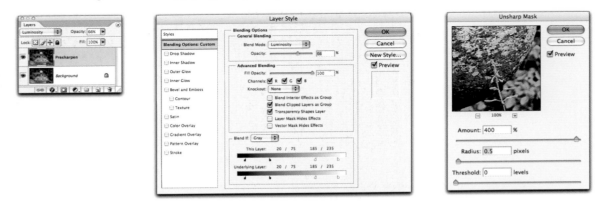

I create a sharpening layer set to Luminosity with 66 percent opacity. Then I set the Blend If sliders to constrain sharpening to the midtones.

I run the Unsharp Mask filter with Amount 400, Radius 0.6, Threshold 0, to produce the result shown below.

Figure 6-30   Applying sharpening for source, *continued*

Detail at 300 ppi   *Zoomed in at 100 percent*

To sharpen for content, I create an edge mask. In this image, the dominant tendency I want to emphasize is the high-frequency detail, so in this case I can omit the step of creating a blur layer and simply blur the layer mask instead—this example is right on the edge of where the Find Edges filter needs a blur layer and where it does not.

So I use Calculations to create a channel that will serve as the basis for the edge mask. I run the Find Edges filter, invert the channel to get light edges instead of dark ones, and do a small-radius blur with Gaussian Blur before loading the channel as a selection and applying it to the sharpening layer as a mask. Once the mask is loaded, I delete the alpha channel since it's no longer needed, then I sharpen with Unsharp Mask.

Figure 6-31 shows the process of creating the mask and sharpening for content, along with the results it produces.

Figure 6-31 Applying sharpening for content

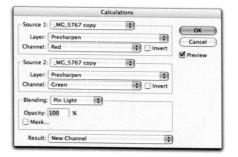

I use Calculations to create a new channel directly from the sharpening layer, which will serve as the basis for the edge mask.

The new channel

The new channel after Find Edges

After Invert

Figure 6-31 Applying sharpening for content, *continued*

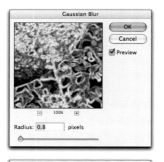

I use Gaussian Blur to blur the mask lightly, then I load the channel as a selection, and apply it to the sharpening layer as a layer mask.

With the layer mask in place, I target the sharpening layer and run Unsharp Mask with Amount 200, Radius 0.6, Threshold 0, to produce the results shown below.

After blurring

Sharpened for content, 300 ppi

Sharpened for content, 100 percent zoom

The image can benefit from some localized work. I employ the edge-protected smoothing brush described in "Smoothing Brushes" in Chapter 5 to blur the distracting background foliage slightly. Then I use the texture brush described in "Special Sharpening Brushes" in Chapter 5 to emphasize the texture of the stone.

Figure 6-32 shows the image before localized work, after the background blurring, and after the application of the texture brush.

After the localized adjustments, the image can now be archived as a use-neutral master, and sharpened for output at different sizes and resolutions. Figure 6-33 shows the image after output sharpening for a downsampled version, and for a detail at the image's native resolution, using the same output sharpening routine I've used throughout this book.

Figure 6-32   Localized adjustments

Before local adjustments

Figure 6-32   Localized adjustments, *continued*

After blurring the background

After the texture brush

Figure 6-33   Sharpened for output

Figure 6-33 Sharpened for output, *continued*

Sweating the Details

The way we handle image detail is every bit as important to the final appearance of our images as is the way we handle tone and color. Yet detail control has, thus far in the short history of digital imaging, received far less attention than those other, admittedly crucial, aspects of imaging.

For years, I like most practioners did sharpening as an ad hoc, seat-of-the-pants procedure until the realization slowly dawned that by flailing around trying different sharpening tricks, I often created extra work and produced results that, while acceptable, weren't nearly as good as they should be.

In evangelizing the workflow approach to sharpening that I've taken throughout this book, my goal has been to educate and inform, but also to move the discussion forward. I don't claim to have all the answers, but I hope you've found useful the ones I do have.

Index